Demand is insatiable! First there was *Rugby Jokes*, then came *Son of Rugby Jokes*, *More Rugby Jokes*, *What Rugby Jokes Did Next*, *Even More Rugby Jokes* and *Rugby Jokes Score Again*. Now, a seventh collection of earthy humour has been culled from Britain's rugby fans in *Hands Up For Rugby Jokes*. And don't forget to look out for *Rugby Songs* and *More Rugby Songs*.

Hands Up
For Rugby Jokes

Illustrated by Raymond Turvey

SPHERE BOOKS LIMITED

SPHERE BOOKS LIMITED

Published by the Penguin Group
27 Wrights Lane, London W8 5TZ, England
Viking Penguin Inc., 40 West 23rd Street, New York, New York 10010, USA
Penguin Books Australia Ltd, Ringwood, Victoria, Australia
Penguin Books Canada Ltd, 2801 John Street, Markham, Ontario, Canada L3R 1B4
Penguin Books (NZ) Ltd, 182-190 Wairau Road, Auckland 10, New Zealand

Penguin Books Ltd, Registered Offices: Harmondsworth, Middlesex, England

First published in Great Britain in 1988 by Sphere Books Ltd
Copyright © E. L. Ranelagh 1988

Printed and bound in Great Britain by
Richard Clay Ltd, Bungay, Suffolk

Contents

Wimmen

A NEW ELEMENT

Symbol: Woe
Name: Woman
Accepted Weight: 120
Physical Properties: Boils at nothing and freezes at any minute. Melts when properly treated; very bitter if not well used.
Occurrence: Found wherever man exists.
Chemical Properties: Possesses great affinity for gold, silver, platinum, and precious stones. Violent reaction if alone. Turns green when placed beside a better-looking specimen.
Uses: Highly ornamental; useful as a tonic in the acceleration of low spirits and as an equalizer of the distribution of wealth. Probably the most effective income-reducing agent known.
CAUTION: HIGHLY EXPLOSIVE IN INEXPERIENCED HANDS.

OH!

Lily couldn't imagine why she was so popular.
'Is it my lovely hair?' she asked a friend.
'No.'
'Is it my cute figure?'
'No.'
'My personality?'
'No.'
'Then I give up.'
'That's it!'

GRIEVANCE

A man snatches the first kiss, pleads for the second, demands the third, takes the fourth, accepts the fifth – and endures all the rest.

MORE GRIEVANCE

'It was terrible!' reported the pretty teenager to her girl-friend. 'I had to change my seat four times at the films.'
'Some man bother you?'
'Yes,' said the girl. 'Finally.'

GRIEVANCE?

Bill rushed into his fiancée's bedroom and tried to rape her. She began screaming at him angrily.

'Two words,' he pleaded. 'Let me say two words!'

After using all the insults she knew, she finally said, 'All right, all right. What are your two words, you dirty bum!'

'Let go.'

A NEW PROBLEM

One woman to another: 'What do you think – my husband came home from the office yesterday and told me he bought a condominium!'

'That's nice. But if I were you, I'd still take the pill.'

AN OLD ONE

Elderly Miss Barrett called the police station to report the indecent behaviour of her neighbour.

'Exactly what has he done?' asked the policeman.

'Every morning when he passes my house,' she said indignantly, 'he deliberately whistles dirty songs! Like this one!'

'I'd like you to kiss me,' she said,
'Between my toes . . . please bend your head.
Not there! Oh, no. No.
It tickles me so!
Between the two big ones, instead.'

DESCRIPTIONS OF WOMEN

In the USA, the early champions of women's rights were by Act of Congress permitted to dress as males.

Mark Twain saw one of these first feminists in ill-fitting trousers and a wrinkled coat. He remarked, 'That lady is a perfect example of a SELF-MADE MAN.'

AND THIS?

She was a loose-fitting woman in a tight-fitting dress.

AND

Love is supposed to be blind, but lots of fellows can see twice as much in their sweethearts as I can.

OVERHEARD

I was judging a beauty contest the other day and got there early.

From a room nearby I could hear one of the girls having her chest measured.

'Well, Dora,' said the lucky chap with the tape, 'that's very good – 41 inches.'

My mouth watered!

And then the chap said, 'Now let's measure the other one!'

FAVOURITE DRINK

A French eggnog – 2 eggs yolks, 2 teaspoons of sugar, and 4 jiggers of cognac in a tall, warm lass.

OVERHEARD IN THE WOODS

A rather one-sided conversation which went as follows:

'I certainly will not! Mother said I shouldn't! And anyway, the grass is too damp. Besides, £5 isn't enough!'

DANCING?

Selena was dancing when her brooch became unfastened.

She asked her escort to retrieve it.

Somewhat embarrassed but happy to help her, he reached cautiously down the back of her dress. After a moment he said, 'Awfully sorry! But I can't seem to locate it.'

'Try further down,' she suggested.

He did, though he was beginning to blush. Still no brooch.

'Down still further,' she ordered.

He noticed that they were now being watched by every couple on the dance floor. He blushed a deep red and said, 'I feel a perfect ass!'

'Never mind that!' she snapped. 'Just get the brooch.'

WAR GAMES

During the war, the motto of the Women's Land Army was 'Back to the Land'.

The soldiers told them they had it wrong. They explained that the order for girls was 'Backs to the Land', and gallantly offered to show them how to do it.

SANTA CLAUS

One Christmas Eve, Santa came sliding down the chimney to fill the children's stockings. Instead of stockings, he found a beautiful naked lady lying by the fireplace.

The lady said, 'Santa, Santa, stay with me!'

Santa said, 'Sorry, madam, but the reindeer are stamping on the roof and the sled is full. Time's short. I have to go.'

The lady said, 'Santa, Santa, let the reindeer wait and stay with me!'

Santa said, 'And what about the children round the world, expecting their toys?'

She said, 'Santa darling, for just a little while forget the children! Come up close and stay with me!'

Santa said, 'Oh well, I may as well stay. I'll never make it back up the chimney this way.'

SOB STORY

A young lady in the waiting room of an airport was crying steadily. Seeing her tears, a young man came over and tried to soothe her. He put a comforting arm around her and talked to her. When she continued to weep, he squeezed her tighter. 'Isn't there anything I can do,' he asked, 'to make you stop crying?'

'I'm afraid not,' the girl sobbed. 'It's hay fever. But please keep on trying.'

REASONS WHY A BEER IS BETTER THAN A WOMAN

1 You can enjoy a beer anytime during the month. •
2 Beer stains wash out.
3 You don't have to wine and dine a beer.
4 Your beer will always wait patiently in the car for you when you play sports.
5 When a beer goes flat, you can throw it away.
6 A beer is never late.
7 Hangovers go away.
8 A beer doesn't get jealous when you grab another beer.
9 A beer never gets a headache.
10 When you go to a bar, you know you can always pick up another beer.
11 After a beer, the bottle is still worth five pence.
12 A beer won't get upset when you come home with another beer on your breath.
13 If you pour a beer right, you'll always get a good head.
14 You can have more than one beer a night and not feel guilty.
15 You can share a beer with your friends.
16 A beer always goes down easy.
17 You always know that you're the first one to pop a beer.
18 A beer is always wet.
19 A beer never demands equality.
20 You can have a beer in public.
21 You don't have to wash a beer before it tastes good.
22 Beer lids come off without a fight.

A MAID, I DARE NOT TELL

A maid, I dare not tell her name
For fear I should disgrace her,
Tempted a young man for to come
One night, and to embrace her;
But at the door he made a stop,
He made a stop, he made a stop,
    But she lay still, but sleeping said,
    'The latch pull up, the latch pull up.'

This young man, hearing of her words,
Pulled up the latch and entered;
And in the place unfortunately,
To her mother's bed he ventured.
The poor maid was sore afraid
And almost dead, and almost dead,
    But she lay still, and sleeping said,
    'The truckle-bed, the truckle-bed.'

Unto the truckle-bed he went;
But as the youth was going
Th' unlucky cradle stood in's way
And almost spoiled his wooing.
After that, the maid he spied,
The maid he spied, the maid he spied,
    But she lay still, and sleeping said,
    'The other side, the other side.'

Unto the other side he went
To show the love he meant her,
Pulled off his clothes courageously
And fell to the work he was sent for.
But the poor maid made no reply,
Made no reply, made no reply,
    But she lay still, and sleeping said,
    'A little too high, a little too high.'

This lusty lover was half ashamed
Of her gentle admonition.
He thought to charge her home as well
As any girl could wish him.
'O now, my love, I'm right, I know,
I'm right, I know, I'm right, I know.'
    But she lay still, and sleeping said,
    'A little too low, a little too low.'

Though by mistakes, at length this youth
His business so well tended,
He hit the mark so cunningly
He defied the world to mend it.
'O now, my love, I'm right, I swear,
I'm right, I swear, I'm right, I swear.'
    But she lay still, and speaking said,
    'O there, O there, O there, O there.'

SO THAT'S WHAT YOU CALL WALTZING, MATILDA?

Once a jolly swagman knocked upon a kitchen door,
Up jumped the house-wife, 'Now who can that be?'
'Good morning, Mr Swagman, come into my billabong,
'You'll come a-waltzing, Matilda, with me.'

Chorus:
Waltzing Matilda, waltzing Matilda,
You'll come a-waltzing, Matilda, with me.
Never mind your boomerang, come into my billabong
You'll come a-waltzing, Matilda, with me.

'Now what can I do for such a handsome man as you?
I'm all alone in the house,' said she.
'Would you care to stow your jumbuck in to my tuckerbag?
You'll come a-waltzing, Matilda, with me.'

'Too right,' said the swagman, but just then his billy boiled.
In rushed her husband, one, two, three;
He clobbered the swagman, grabbed him by the coolabahs,
'You'll come a-waltzing, Matilda, with me.'

And that was the end of a very handsome thoroughbred,
The moral of the story's plain for all to see;
Never stuff your jumbuck in someone else's tuckerbag,
Just keep a-waltzing, Matilda, with me.

Scoring

WHEW!

'You'd better go! My husband just drove up!'
'Where's the back door?'
'We don't have one!'
'Where would you like one?'

ANSWERS

Candy's dandy.
But liquor's quicker.

or
Candy's dandy.
But sex won't rot your teeth.

QUESTIONS

How do you screw a 500-lb woman?
Cautiously.

or
On top, for sure!

and
How would you describe a man who gets caught in adultery?
Slow.

ECSTASY

How would you describe ecstasy?
   Something that happens between the Scotch and soda and the bacon and eggs.

ECSTASY WITH TRIMMINGS

At the Cup Final at Wembley, a man arrived just a few minutes before the kick-off.
   'Sorry, sir,' said the attendant, 'all I've got now are some seats in the stands – £25 each.'
   '£25!' said the man. 'Why, I could get a woman for that!'
   'Yes,' said the attendant, 'but you wouldn't get ninety minutes and a brass band at the interval, would you?'

TELL THIS TO A WOMAN

According to the Kinsey Report, 90% of oversexed women are [whisper this] *hard of hearing*.

FRANK

In the lobby of a de luxe hotel, a beautiful girl smiled invitingly at a man who seemed to be looking for someone. But he paid no attention.

Finally she said, 'Hello there!'

'Don't bother, ma'am,' he said. 'Liquor is my weakness.'

Things to do today . . .

FRANK AND ERNEST

A man walks into a pub and says to a customer at the bar, 'Can you give us a light?'

He says, 'Bugger off.'

'Look, mate, I only asked for a light.'

'I heard you. Bugger off.'

'Why won't you give me a light, then?'

'Because if I do, you'll buy me a drink. Then I'll have to buy you a drink and then we'll both get drunk. So, go home!'

'I can't go home. I've missed the last bus.'

'Oho! So you'll want me to give you a bed at my house?'

'Well, yeh, maybe.'

'My daughter is a beauty queen. You'll want to sleep with her.'

'Yeh, yeh!'

'And you'll make her pregnant.'

'Yeh!'

'And you won't marry her!'

'Oh yes, I will!'

'Oh no, you won't. Because I'm not giving you a light.'

TALLULAH

Tallulah Bankhead, winner of many awards as a film actress, was famous for her outspoken private life as well.

A male interviewer once asked her, 'With your deep voice, Miss Bankhead, has anyone ever mistaken you for a man?'

'No, darling. Has anyone ever made that mistake with you?'

14

ALAS!

Gentlemen prefer blondes, but they take what they can get.

IT'S *CHARITY* THAT BEGINS AT HOME

This is National Sex Week. If you've already given at the office, you don't need to give it at home.

USED CARS · WHISKEY · PEAT MOSS · NAILS · LAND
FLY SWATTERS · RACING FORMS · BONGO DRUMS

DAVE WRIGHT

WARS FOUGHT	TIGERS TAMED
GOVERNMENTS RUN	SALOONS EMPTIED
BRIDGES DESTROYED	ORGIES ORGANIZED
UPRISINGS QUELLED	VIRGINS CONVERTED
REVOLUTIONS STARTED	COMPUTERS VERIFIED

WHO'S PLAYING

The phone rang and Mike picked it up. 'Hey Mike, this is Jerry. I've got two tickets to the hockey game tonight. Want to go?'

'Thanks,' said Mike, 'but I can't. Wardle's playing tonight.'

A few days later, Jerry tried again. 'Got tickets to a League game tonight. Are you interested?'

'Can't make it,' said Mike. 'Wardle's playing tonight.'

Early the next evening, Jerry tried once more. 'Got two good seats for the fight tonight. How about it?'

'Sorry. Wardle's playing tonight.'

'Wait a second,' said Mike. 'What does this guy Wardle play?'

'I don't know,' said Jerry. 'I never even met him. I don't know what he plays and I don't know where he plays, but when Wardle's playing, I'm screwing around with his wife.'

VERBAL SCORING

An airline passenger with three pieces of luggage went to the check-in desk and put them on the scales.

'Send the big one to Tokyo, the brown bag to Morocco and the blue case to Los Angeles.'

'Sorry, sir,' said the attendant. 'I can't do that.'

'Why not?' asked the passenger. 'You did it last year.'

AND FROM MARK TWAIN

Visiting New Zealand, Mark Twain handed the railway conductor half of his ticket, which was the custom then used with juvenile passengers.

The official looked at Twain's white hair and bushy white moustache and asked, 'And are you a child?'

'No, not any more,' said Mark Twain casually. 'But I was when I got on your damn train.'

AND ACROSS A CROWDED ROOM

The party was a smoothly swinging scene, with all the lights turned low. Joe saw a female form alone in a corner. He slipped up behind her and clasped her in a passionate embrace.

'How dare you!'

'Oh, pardon me. I thought you were my sister.'

'You nitwit! I *am* your sister.'

ANOTHER PARTY

Then there was this Danish diplomat in South America. At a party, he saw a gorgeous creation in red. He crossed over and asked if he could have that dance.

The reply was, 'No.'

'Why?' he asked.

'For three reasons. One, you are Danish. Two, this is the Brazilian national anthem. And three, I am the Cardinal of this country!'

WORLD TRAVELLER

INTERNATIONAL LOVER

RENOWNED GOURMET

LAST OF THE BIG SPENDERS

HEADLINE?

Headless body found in topless bar.

BOTTOM LINE

And there was the girl who wanted to keep as a memento the ring given her by a departing suitor.

'No. You can remember that I refused it to you. I like that better.'

END OF THE LINE

A crowd of presumably ailing people were lined up in front of a new NHS clinic early one morning.

One little man walked past everyone and headed for the front of the line. The first-comers muttered in protest and pushed him back to the end.

The little fellow grumbled to himself and again started for the front. Again he was manhandled to the back.

He tried a third time and this time he was hoisted bodily and thrown back – fists flying on all sides.

He got up, dusted himself and thundered, 'Just push me back once more – and I won't open the clinic!'

RONNIE BARKER SAID

'Here's tomorrow's weather forecast. The sun will be killing 'em in Gillingham, it'll be choking in Woking, dry in Rye and cool in Goole. And if you live in Lissingdown, take an umbrella.'

A SCORE AT LORDS'

Lord X: 'My ancestors came over with William the Conqueror, you know.'

Lord Y: 'Yes. Well, the immigration laws are much stricter now.'

MAE WEST

. . . who topped a compliment when she replied, 'Yes, when
I'm good I'm very good – but when I'm bad I'm better.'

AND LASTLY, DON'T DRINK AND DRIVE

. . . you'll spill it.

A WANTON TRICK

If anyone longs for a musical song,
Although that his hearing be thick,
The sound that it bears will ravish his ears —
'Tis but a wanton trick.

A pleasant young maid on an instrument played
That knew neither note nor prick.
She had a good will to live by her skill —
'Tis but a wanton trick.

A youth in that art, well seen in his part,
They called him Darbyshire Dick,
Came to her a suitor and would be her tutor —
'Tis but a wanton trick.

He pleased her so well that backward she fell
And swooned as though she were sick.
So sweet was his note that up went her coat —
'Tis but a wanton trick.

The string of his viol she put to the trial
'Til she had the full length of the stick.
Her white-bellied lute she set to his flute —
'Tis but a wanton trick.

Thus she with her lute and he with his flute
Held every crotchet and prick.
She learned at her leisure yet paid for her pleasure —
'Tis but a wanton trick.

His viol string burst, her tutor she cursed;
However, she played with the stick.
From October to June she was quite out of tune —
'Tis but a wanton trick.

And then she repented that e'er she consented
To have either note or prick;
For learning so well made her belly to swell —
'Tis but a wanton trick.

All maids that make trial of a lute or a viol,
Take heed how you handle the stick;
If you like not this order, come, try my recorder —
'Tis but a wanton trick.

A NUMBER OF TRADESMEN

A number of tradesmen one day did combine
  With a rum-ti dum, tum-ti dum terro,
To the best of their skill to make something divine,
  With a row-de dow, row-de dow derro.

The first was a Carpenter, he thought it fit,
  With a rum-ti-dum, etc.
With a bony broad axe to give it a slit.
  With a row-de dow, etc.

The next was a Mercer, so neat and so trim.
  With a rum-ti dum, etc.
And he with red satin did line it within,
  With a row-de dow, etc.

Then in came a Furrier, so bold and so stout,
  With a rum-ti dum, etc.
And he with a bear-skin did fur it about,
  With a row-de dow, etc.

The Fishmonger next, and he was full bent,
  With a rum-ti dum, etc.
With ling and red herring to give it a scent,
  With a row-de dow, etc.

Then in came a Parson, so bold and so hot,
  With his rum-ti dum, etc.
So to make it all Christian he called it a trot.
  With a row-de dow, etc.

Marriage

THESE DAYS

A couple wearing scarecrow hair of many colours, bilious sweaters and torn jeans went to an exclusive restaurant for dinner. But their punk appearance annoyed the doorman.

He said, 'You have to wear a tie before we can admit you to the Regency Room.'

One of the punks disappeared for a short time and returned wearing a tie.

The doorman went over to him, and pointed to the other. 'How about him?'

The one with the tie said, 'Idiot, that's my wife!'

DOROTHY PARKER SAID:

A couple who had been living together for many years finally decided to get married, and the eager bride bored all her friends talking about this great event.

That's when Dorothy Parker, an old acquaintance, sent the following immortal telegram:

'Congratulations! So what's new?'

HABIT-FORMING

Logan returned late one night from a month-long business trip and lay down beside his wife, who was dreaming that she was making love to her boyfriend. Soon he fell asleep.

Suddenly in her dream, Mrs Logan imagined she heard a familiar step outside the bedroom door.

'Oh my God!' she cried aloud in her sleep. 'Get out, my husband's coming!'

So Logan leapt up and out of bed and ran to the closet.

SAME AGAIN

Maxwell arrived home unexpectedly and found his wife lying in bed. He looked suspiciously at a cigar smouldering in the ash-tray beside the bed.

'Where did that cigar come from?' he demanded.

The bathroom door opened and a shaky masculine voice said, 'Cuba!'

NOT QUITE THE SAME

Smith discovered his wife in bed with another man.

'What's the meaning of this?' he demanded. 'Who is this guy?'

'That seems a fair question,' said his wife, rolling over. 'What's your name, fella?'

SIMILAR

'That's a lovely suit you're wearing, Bob.'

'Yes, it was a surprise present from the missus.'

'A surprise, was it?'

'Indeed it was. I came home early one night and found it lying on the bed.'

DAFFYNITION

Polygamy is having more wives than you need.
Monogamy is the same thing.

TRUE PERSPECTIVE

Larry came back from a business trip a day ahead of time – and found his wife in bed with his best friend.

He was dumbfounded. 'Pete,' he said, 'I'm married to her, so I've *got* to! But you?'

AND

Bob was telling a friend about his wife's birthday on the previous day.

'I gave her a diamond pin, and then took her to a show, with a fancy dinner in between.'

The friend smiled. 'And after that,' he said, 'I bet there was plenty of loving.'

'Not on your life!' said Bob. 'I did more than enough for her as it was.'

REVERSE PROCEDURE

The painter answered his model's knock on his studio door with a passionate kiss.

But glancing out the window, he added, 'Quick, get your clothes off! Here comes my wife!'

FRIGIDITY

The new husband asked his doctor's advice on a most intimate matter.

'It's my Kathie, doctor,' he said. 'You know a sweeter girl doesn't exist, but she doesn't seem to take kindly to . . . well, she doesn't want to . . . I mean, um, you know what I mean, doctor.'

'You mean love-making, Tom?'

'Well, yes, that is what I mean.'

'I'm not surprised that Kathie is a little diffident in this respect. I knew her mother – she was a frigid woman. I'd be prepared to bet that she'd passed on her dislike of sex to her daughter.'

'But what can I do?'

'Kathie is a healthy, normal girl, and there is no reason why she shouldn't enjoy a normal relationship with you. I know she loves you, and she only needs a little shove to do what comes naturally. Tell you what, why don't you take her by surprise, when she is least expecting it? Once you've done the deed and she realizes it isn't so terrible, why, everything will be fine. I'm sure of it.'

'Okay, doctor. Thank you, doctor. I'll give it a try.'

Three weeks later Tom came into the doctor's office, beaming all over and bursting with the joy of living, a changed man.

'It looks as if you've solved your problems, eh?' asked the doctor.

'Yes, I certainly have, doctor,' said the happy young man, 'and I can't begin to thank you enough.'

'Tell me about it.'

'Well, I did just what you said. We were having a bite to eat one Saturday, and I got to thinking about what you said. There we were sitting at the table, eating and not saying much, and I thought to myself, "She'll never expect me to make a grab at her now!" So that's just what I did! I grabbed her and before she knew what was up, I was! Right there and then, on the table! And just as you said, since then everything's been great between us.'

'That's just fine, Tom. I'm very happy for you both.'

'There's just one thing . . .'

'Yes?'

'They won't let us eat in MacDonald's any more.'

FERTILITY

What's the difference between knowledge and faith?

Mrs Hunt says she has three children – that's knowledge.

Mr Hunt says he has three children – that's faith.

AND IN WALES

Jones the Post: 'Have you heard the news, Dai boyo? Evans Williams is getting married to that girlfriend of his.'

Dai the Dairy: 'Married? I didn't even know she was expecting!'

Jones the Post: 'She isn't.'

Dai the Dairy: 'Getting married and not expecting? Boyo, that's *posh*!'

WEDDING LINES

Toast: 'To our wives and sweethearts! May they never meet!'

Commiseration: 'He got his wedding-tackle shot off!'

Plain Truth: 'Beneath my husband's cold hard exterior – there's a cold hard interior.'

BROODING

Macdowell was brooding over his beer in the bar and said to his friend, 'I tell you, I don't know what I'm going to do about my wife!'

'What is it now?'

'The same old thing – money. She's always asking for money! Only last Thursday she wanted £50. Yesterday she asked for £100. And this morning, if you please, she demanded £200!'

'What does she do with all that money, for heaven's sake?'

'There's no way of finding out. I never give her any.'

NAME-DROPPING

Johnson met an old friend for the first time in years. 'Richards, how are you? I hear you've become very rich.'

'I can't complain,' said Richards. 'I've a flat in the city, an estate in the country, two Rolls Royces, a wife and three children. I own several companies and I've some good investments.'

'Sounds great,' said Johnson, 'but after all, what can you do that I can't do? We both eat and sleep and drink. What else is there in life?'

'You call that living? I get up, have a fine breakfast, then I lie on my verandah. After that I play a round of golf and come back with a good appetite for lunch. Lunch over, I lie on my verandah again, and if I feel like it, have the chauffeur drive me in a Rolls to one conference or another. In the evening I have a splendid dinner, lie on my verandah again, and later go on to a party or the theatre.'

'That's wonderful! And all without work!' marvelled Johnson.

That night at home, Johnson told his wife about Richards. When he mentioned Richards' wife and three children, Mrs Johnson interrupted.

'What's his wife's name?' she asked.

'I don't know,' he said. 'I think it's Veranda.'

COMMON COMPLAINT

The lady of the house: 'And tell me, why did you leave your last position?'
New maid: 'The children were too backward and the father was too forward.'

UNCOMMON

An official in the Welfare Office was interviewing an applicant who asked for financial assistance for herself and thirteen children.

He checked the papers in her file once again. 'I don't understand,' he said. 'I thought you said that your husband left you over ten years ago, yet eight of your children are under ten years old.'

'Oh, I can explain!' said the applicant cheerfully. 'You see, he comes back now and again to apologize!'

IN COMMON

Two men were walking down the street when one suddenly grabbed the other's arm and said, 'Quick! In here!'

They dodged into the lobby of a hotel. The second man said, 'What on earth's the matter?'

'Look over there on the other side of the street,' said the first man. 'It's my wife – and she's talking to my girlfriend!'

The second man glanced through the hotel's glass doors and said, 'Good Lord! You're right! Except that it's my wife talking to my girlfriend!'

MARRIAGE IN THE OLD DAYS

A man was asked by his neighbour how his sick wife was.

'Indeed, neighbour, the case is pitiful. My wife fears she shall die and I fear she will not die, which between us make a very sad house.'

A man wished all cuckolds in the seas.
  Then answered him
His fair young wife, 'Sir, for your ease,
  Learn first to swim.'

As the mourners were walking to his wife's funeral, the husband called out, 'Don't go so fast. Why need we make a toil of pleasure?'

A husband to his wife, 'By this candle, I dreamed last night that I was a cuckold.'

To which, wide-eyed, she answered, 'Husband, by this bread, you are not!'

He said, 'Wife, eat the bread you have sworn on.'

She said, 'Then you must first eat the candle!'

AND TODAY

A young fellow was very warmly pursuing a married woman.

'Leave me alone!' she said. 'I have a husband who won't thank you for making him a cuckold.'

'No,' he replied, 'but you will, I hope.'

Early in the morning a young bride saw her husband beginning to get out of bed.

'My darling!' she said. 'Are you getting up already? Do lie down a little longer and rest yourself.'

'No, my dear,' he replied. 'I'll get up and rest myself.'

An elderly wife inquired, 'Did you miss me while I was gone?'

The husband replied, 'Were you gone?'

And another wife asked, 'Will you still love me when I'm old and fat and ugly?'

He said, 'I do, don't I?'

'I realise that this is only a formality,' said the young man to his girlfriend's father, 'but I would like to ask you for your daughter's hand in marriage.'

'Where did you get the idea it was only a formality?'

'From her obstetrician.'

Father and son were enjoying a nightcap on the night before Joe's wedding. Lifting his glass in a toast to his father, Joe asked, 'Any advice before I take the big step, Dad?'

'Yes,' the father said. 'Two things. First, insist on having one night out each week with the boys. Second, don't waste it on the boys.'

MOTHER-IN-LAW

A burglar broke into my mother-in-law's flat, but all he took was one look.

'Steve, you're a really good man,' a friend remarked to him. 'You let your mother-in-law live in your house with your own family all those years, and she wouldn't even speak to you!'
    Steve replied, 'That was the only thing that kept me from leaving.'

Les Dawson's mother-in-law stepped on to a Speak-Your-Weight weighing machine.
    It said, 'One at a time, *please*!'

What is the penalty for bigamy?
    Two mothers-in-law.

Girl to boyfriend: My mother thinks you're effeminate.
Boyfriend: Well, compared with her, I suppose I am.

CAR STICKER

Baby on board – mother-in-law in trunk.

Marriage is like a hot bath.
Once you're in it, it's not so hot.

A RIDDLE

My pretty maid, fain would I know
What thing it is 'twill breed delight;
That strive to stand, that cannot go,
That feeds the mouth that cannot bite.

It is a pretty pricking thing,
A pleasing and a standing thing;
It was the truncheon Mars did use,
A bedward bit that maidens choose.

It is a friar with a bald head,
A staff to beat a cuckold dead;
It is a gun that shoots point-blank,
It hits betwixt a maiden's flank.

It is a shaft of Cupid's cut,
'Twill serve to rove, to prick, to butt;
'Twas ne'er a maid but by her will
Will keep it in her quiver still.

It has a head much like a mole's
And yet it loves to creep in holes.
The fairest maid that e'er took life
For love of this became a wife.

Boyfriends

ONCE UPON A TIME

Once upon a time there was a king who had two daughters. One was the most beautiful girl in the kingdom, but the other was the ugliest girl in the kingdom. Now in the land there was a terrible dragon. Every year it demanded a maiden as a sacrifice, or otherwise it would destroy everyone in the country.

The year had come when it was the king's turn to provide the sacrifice. He had to choose from his own family, so one daughter or the other had to go. The king loved them equally, and he didn't know what to do. So he sent messengers to all the princes in neighbouring countries to help him.

His letter said, 'Slay the dragon and I will give you my most beautiful daughter in marriage, or I will give you the other one and my kingdom as well.'

One of the princes, a famous fighter, replied that he would fight the wicked dragon. He went to the rock where it always came for the sacrifice of the year, and after a long battle he killed it.

There were great celebrations in the kingdom, and the prince went to the palace to claim his reward.

Now guess, who did the prince take?

The king, of course. Remember this is a fairy tale.

HAVE YOU HEARD ABOUT...

The antique dealer who spent his time stripping the dressers and French-polishing the tall-boys?

QUIZ

Q. What do you call an Irish queer?
A. Gay-lick.

Q. What do you call a Spanish queer?
A. Senorita.

Q. What do you call a Jewish queer?
A. He-blew.

ROBIN HOOD AND HIS MF MEN

Robin Hood and his band of men were in Sherwood Forest. As was their custom, they had gathered round the fire in the dark of night to plan an attack on the Sheriff's castle.

When the time and method of the attack were settled, Robin felt that his band needed an extra pep talk. So he got up in front of them and waved his arm for silence.

'Come on, men,' he cried. 'Let's rally, rally, rally!'

The men yelled back. 'Right, you lead, we'll follow!'

'Rally, rally, rally!' cried Robin. 'What are we going to do? We're going to storm the castle and rape the men and pillage the women!'

'Rape the *men* and pillage the *women*?' one of the boys asked.

'Yes, we're going to rape the men and pillage the women!'

'Did he say, rape the men and pillage the women?'

Then Little John – all six and a half feet of him – got up, and he said, 'I say, Robin, don't you mean rape the *women* and pillage the *men*?'

And from the back of the group, a little voice spoke up: 'Wobin's the boss! Wobin's the boss!'

MODERN ROBIN

Jesse James was going to rob a train. As usual, while his gang kept their guns on the passengers, he told everyone what he was going to do.

'Before we start, I'm going to fill you in, all you people, on what we're planning. We're going to rape all you men and rob all you women.'

One fella stood up. 'Don't you have that in reverse, Jesse? You mean you're goin' to rape all the women and rob all the men.'

A little fag in the back called out, 'You let Jesse do what she wants to do!'

SAME IDEA

There was this butcher who went to Stockholm for a sex change operation. It cost him £75,000 and left him without a sausage.

He'd have been better off having his operation in London' – Just snip, snip, snip, and Bob's your Auntie!'

MIGHTY LIKE A ROSE

Sweetest little fellow,
Wears his mother's clothes
Don't know what to call him
But I think he's one of those.

DRESS SENSE

As he climbed on the bus, an obviously gay guy was sneered at by the driver.

'Hi, faggot,' the driver said. 'Where are your pearls?'

'Pearls with corduroy!' shrieked the gay. 'Are you *mad*?'

ALL CORRECT

At an international Air Show, a flyer in an RAF plane bales out. He just gets his parachute open when a flyer from another plane comes down, but this man's chute doesn't open.

As he's falling past, the first flyer catches him and they descend together.

The first man says, 'Hello.'

The second replies, 'Hello.'

'British?'

'Certainly.'

'Labour Party?'

'Conservative.'

'Oxford?'

'Cambridge.'

'Homosexual?'

'Certainly not!'

'Pity' – he drops him.

BOYS IN THE BAND

A man had heard various friends describing their healthy holidays at nudist camps, and so he decided to try one himself.

The resort he chose was certainly in a beautiful area, and he was looking forward to long walks in the forest as in the days of his childhood. So as soon as his holiday started he went to the nudist camp and the very next morning he went for a walk in the woods. All was as he'd hoped. But then he noticed a sign nailed to a tree: Beware of the homosexuals.

'Well, what do you know!' he said to himself. But he wasn't worried. 'I can manage them,' he said. 'I've done it before.'

He went on. He came to a second notice, much smaller than the first, on another tree: Look out! Danger of homosexuals!

He began to get a bit worried. Was this part of the life at a nudist camp?

Then he saw another notice. It was a tiny one, with very small print. He walked up to it and bent down to read: We warned you . . .

GRAFITTI

'Hello! I am a fairy. My name is Nuff. Fairy Nuff.'

If God had wanted homosexuality, He would have created Adam and Steve.

On a condom-vending machine: 'Don't buy this chewing gum. It tastes horrid.'

'My mother made me a homosexual.'
   'If I give her the wool, will she make me one too?'

TROUBLES

Two men in the fashion business were discussing their sons. The first one said sadly, 'My son is no good. He just lounges around the office all day and chases after models.'

The second said with a heavy sigh, 'You think you have troubles! My son too. He hangs around all day and kisses all the models.'

'Why is that so much worse than my son?'

'I'm in men's wear.'

BOYFRIENDS

'Can a couple of homosexual men produce a baby?'

'No, but they can have a lot of fun trying.'

SEQUEL

Two queens were talking. One said, 'Well, at least you know who the father is, don't you?'

The other said, 'What? You think I've got eyes in the back of my head?'

SOUTH PACIFIC

Bill Murray and six young women were the only survivors after a shipwreck in the Pacific. They had somehow managed to make it to an uninhabited island.

The island was a paradise – delightful climate, plenty of food and water – and the seven made themselves comfortable. Bill found it ideal, for it was the most natural thing in the world for him to supply affection to each of the six women. They took it in turns – each one had a particular weekday.

But to his surprise, after a while, his duties became burdensome. He began to value his day off more and more.

On one of his days off, he was sitting wearily on the beach, gazing out to sea. He spotted a dot on the horizon. Could it be a ship? Could it mean rescue? He jumped up and waved vigorously.

The speck came nearer and nearer and turned out to be a tiny raft with a single man on board. Another wreck? Another survivor? Bill swallowed his disappointment. But at least it was another man who could take over half the six-fold duties.

As the raft came closer, the man was revealed to be a willowy fellow with delicate features who waved limply and called out, 'I thay, I'm tho glad to thee you!'

And Bill said, 'Well, there go my Sundays.'

TEXAS

The only safe time to go out in Dallas is at 11 o'clock on a Sunday morning. The Mexicans haven't got their cars started yet. The Blacks are all in jail. The Baptists are all in church.

And the Boys are all at brunch.

DID YOU EVER HEAR ABOUT ...

The two Scottish queers: Ben Doon and Phil McCavity?

DER VOGELVERKÄUFER

You're Never too Old and
You're Never too Young

A STICKLER

'How is your grandfather enjoying the retirement home?'
   'Fine, doctor. I don't know what he's been up to, but he's already got three notches on his walking-stick . . .'

A STICKLER FOR GRAMMAR

Bobby's mother had been away for a few weeks and was questioning her small son about events during her absence.
   'Well, one night we had a thunderstorm, and I was scared. So Daddy and me slept together.'
   'Bobby,' said the boy's pretty young nursemaid, 'You mean, "Daddy and I".'
   'No,' said Bobby. 'That was last Thursday. I'm talking about Monday night.'

THE WEIGHT OF AGE

You can tell it's going to be a rotten day when . . . your birthday cake collapses from the weight of the candles.

TOO LATE

The Duke, one of the wealthiest of England's nobility, got married at a very advanced age. His bride was a sweet young thing of eighteen.

On their wedding night as they were preparing for bed, the Duke said, 'Tell me, my dear – did your mother explain to you the – er – the facts of life?'

'No, she didn't,' said his bride shyly.

'Dashed awkward, that,' said His Grace. 'I'm afraid I've forgotten them!'

NOT FUSSY

A small boy went into a chemist's and whispered to the man that he wanted some condoms.

'What size? And who are they for?'

'Gimme assorted sizes,' he said, and explained, 'They're for my sister, she's going on holiday.'

TOO MANY

Gibson, who was seventy, was getting married for the sixth time. As he waited in church for the wedding to begin, he thought of the varied music played at his previous marriages.

The first time, he'd been twenty. The band played 'There'll be a Hot Time in the Old Town Tonight'.

When he took his second wife at age thirty, it was to the tune 'I'll be Loving You Always'.

At forty, they played 'Now and Then'.

At fifty, the song was 'I Don't Get Around Much Any More'.

When he was sixty, and marrying for the fifth time, the music was 'The Thrill is Gone'.

His thoughts were interrupted by the church organ. He walked down the aisle as the organist played, 'Remember When'.

NOT ENOUGH

An old fellow was reminiscing for a reporter.

'Old age runs in my family,' he said. 'My father died when he was 102.'

'Oh, really? But there's nothing unusual in that.'

'And my Grand-Da died when he was 104.'

'Well, that's better — but not quite noteworthy.'

'My Great-Grandfather, he died when he was over 106!'

'Now, that's really something. But was there anything unusual in it?'

'No. It was just because he'd got married when he was 105.'

SPEAKING OF OLD MEN

Frustration is the first time you discover you can't do it the second time.

Panic is the second time you discover you can't do it the first time.

Grandad was asked how he felt about having reached the age of seventy.

'To tell you the truth,' he said, 'I'm not pleased, but it's better than the alternative.'

Although his eyes were riveted on the undressed chorus girls in the night club, the eager senior citizen sighed.

'They don't make 'em like they used to,' he said sadly. 'Or at least I don't.'

*'Goddam you Charlie Brown!, I will not sink if you **take it out**!'*

AND SPEAKING OF OLD WOMEN

After an evening at a rather risqué farce, an elderly couple were going to bed when the old man felt a touch of an urge that he rarely experienced these days.

'Come on, Dora, let's have a party!'

'Go ahead,' she said.

Next morning when they woke she asked him with considerable interest, 'How did you make out last night, John?'

The great-great-grandmother looked at the newborn baby with obvious satisfaction.

'It's a boy!' she said, '– if my memory doesn't fail me.'

COMING OF AGE

Now that their son was sixteen, the wife told her husband that he'd better tell him the facts of life. 'Tell him about the birds and the bees and all that.'

The father said, 'OK. I'll have a talk with him.'

That night he called junior into the living-room.

'Son, now that you're sixteen your mother feels that we should have a talk about the facts of life. Remember when we went to the beach last year on holiday?'

'Yes, Dad.'

'Remember the two girls we met on the beach?'

'Yes, Dad.'

'And remember that night we took them back to their hotel?'

'Yes, Dad.'

'And remember what happened after that?'

'Yes, Dad.'

'Well, it's the same with the birds and the bees.'

SOLDIERING ON

Recently a friend whose hobby is archery moved to Aldershot, where his family settled in happily.

When the six-year-old son joined the local school that autumn, the other boys naturally asked him if his father was with the armed forces.

'I think he used to be,' the boy replied. 'He still has his bows and arrows.'

AND

A couple who had been married for seventy years announced to their friends that they were getting a divorce.

'Good Lord!' exclaimed one friend, turning to the husband, 'You're ninety-five!' And turning to the wife, 'You're ninety! Why are you getting divorced *now*?'

'Oh,' they replied. 'We thought we'd wait until the children were dead.'

AN APPLE A DAY

Johnny came running into the room and asked, 'Dad, may I have another apple?'

His father looked up from his newspaper and glanced at the boy.

'An apple, again?' he demanded. 'Listen, where do you think these apples come from? You think they grow on trees?'

PROBLEMS OF THE ELDERLY

'How can you be sure you'll be remembered after death?'
  'Leave many debts.'

Two old fellows were discussing the ravages of time. One burst out with, 'Hell, Sam, now it takes me all night to do what I used to do all night!'

An ancient couple shuffled into the doctor's office.
  'What seems to be the trouble?' asked the doctor.
  'It affects us both, doctor,' said the husband. 'You see, I am impotent!'
  'According to my records,' said the physician, 'you are eighty-five years of age, and your wife is eighty-three. And yet you complain of impotence?'
  'That's right.'
  'Er – when did you first notice the problem?'
  'Last night, and again this morning.'

Another old man went to his doctor. He too complained that he could no longer have sex.
  'How old are you?'
  'Ninety-seven.'
  'And when did you first notice you were impotent?'
  'This morning.'
  'Well, I'm afraid there's little hope for you. You're much too old for this sort of thing.'
  'Well, then, doc,' pleaded the old man, 'give me something to take the ideas out of my mind.'

An elderly man who had postponed a minor operation for some years was eventually persuaded to enter hospital.
  After being bathed by the nurse, he heaved a sigh of relief. 'Well, thank goodness that's over! I've been dreading that operation . . .'

Dear Sir,

I am sure the Homestead Retirement Home has thanked you and the many others who made gifts to the Home that have brought pleasure and comfort to us residents.

But I wish to thank you personally from the bottom of my heart because I am the recepient of the little portable radio which you gave me. I listen to it constantly when I am awake

It has been so much company for me I have wanted a radio of my very own ever since I came to the home to live. We have nice accomodations here and they take very good care of us. there are two of us in each room. My room mate is Martha Nelson. She is 87 & I am 83

Martha has had a radio of her own ever since she came here ten years ago. She kept it so low I could never hear the programs. When I would ask her to turn it up so I could hear the programs too she wouldn't do it. Bless her, she is a sweet old soul and I suppose she just can't help being that way.

Last week she dropped her radio and it broke into many pieces and cannot be repaired. Last night I was listening to the early evening services of the First Methodist Church and those beautiful old hymns I love so much. Martha asked me to turn the radio up higher so she could hear it too, so naturally I told her to go fuck herself.

Again thank you
I am

Dorothy Murdock.

LEARNING TO BREED

In backwoods America an old-timer was explaining to summer tourists why there weren't any children in the neighbourhood.

'It's the young fellers these days,' he said. 'They don't go tom-catting any more. They go to college. Then they marry city girls that have went to college too, so naturally they don't have no children.'

GROWING PAINS

The small boy asks, 'Daddy, are you still growing?'

'No, son. What makes you think so?'

'Because the top of your head is coming through your hair.'

THE VALUE OF EDUCATION

First lad: My father is so rich, he's sending me to Eton and Oxford.

Second: My father's so rich, he's sending me to Harrow and Cambridge.

Third: My father's so rich, he can afford to let me stay ignorant.

AND RELATIVES

'What's the matter?' the bartender asked a well-dressed young man who seemed morose.

'Two months ago my grandfather died and left me £100,000.'

'Doesn't sound like anything to be glum about,' said the bartender, polishing a glass. 'It should happen to me!'

'Yeah,' said the young man. 'But last month an uncle on the other side died. He left me £500,000.'

'Then why are you so unhappy?'

'This month, so far, not a penny!'

AND FRENCH LESSONS

'What's that, Marie?' the little boy asked the au pair, as he pointed at the elephant.

The zoo's elephant was busy peeing.

'You mean ze trunk?'

'No, that thing down the middle.'

'Oh, you mean ze tail.'

'No, no, that thing there,' the child insisted, pointing straight at it.

'Oh zat, zat is nothing!'

A Frenchman who was standing nearby tipped his hat. 'Mademoiselle is *blasée*,' he said, bowing.

WORDS OF COMFORT

Sixty is a good age for a man.
   If she says yes, he's flattered.
   If she says no, he's relieved.

AND ADVICE

A father sat his son down for some fatherly advice.

'My boy, while it is no longer believed that constant masturbation will lead to insanity or blindness – we see that now as a delusion of the Victorian age – you should know that according to the latest medical opinion, masturbation can be the cause of a serious reduction in hearing.'

'What?' said the boy.

BACK CHAT

'I don't think much of your new girlfriend,' said a father to his son one evening.

'Well,' said the lad, 'she was the best I could pick up with in the old car you've got at the moment.'

'I want a sugar daddy,' she said.

'Yes?'

'With one foot in the grave and the other on a bar of soap.'

RETIREMENT

My nookie days are over,
My pilot light is out.
What used to be my sex appeal
is now my water spout.

Time was when of its own accord,
From my trousers it would spring
But now I have a full time job
To find the blasted thing.

It used to be embarrassing
The way it would behave,
For every single morning,
It would stand and watch me shave.

As old age approaches,
It sure gives me the blues,
To see it hang its withered head
And watch me tie my shoes.

Professions
Laws and Orders

ORDERS

A dinner party was being held in London, and early guests discussed the problem of Northern Ireland while waiting for their host and hostess to appear.

Gradually voices grew louder and tempers shorter until one guest finally said, in the hope of calming things. 'Ah well, there is One Above who alone understands.'

'Yes,' said Mr Thatcher, just arrived, 'and she will be right down.'

MORE ORDERS

In courts and in the language used for judges, the words 'with respect' mean, you're wrong. 'With great respect' means you're seriously wrong. And 'with greatest respect' means, send for the men in white coats.

HIGHEST ORDERS

When decorations are given out, there is the CMG, Companion of the Order of St Michael and St George; the KCMG, Knight Commander of the Order of St Michael and St George; and highest of all, GCMG, Grand Cross of the Order of St Michael and St George.

If these abbreviations are hard to remember, it is suggested that the following may come more easily to mind: Call Me God, Kindly Call Me God, and God Calls Me God.

DISORDERS

At a big social function on a US Air Force base, a young second lieutenant was bored beyond his endurance at the welcoming speech the commanding general was making.

He muttered to the woman at his side, 'What an unbearable old windbag that fellow is!'

The woman turned on him and said, 'Lieutenant, do you know who I am?'

'No, ma'am.'

'I am the wife of that unbearable old windbag, as you call him!'

'Indeed!' said the young lieutenant, drawing himself up. 'And do you know who I am?'

'No, I don't,' said the general's wife.

'Thank God!' breathed the young lieutenant as he melted into the crowd.

ANOTHER DISORDER

At a dinner party, this time it was a doctor who was bored to distraction. Course after course, without interruption, the lady on his right told him all of her symptoms.

Eventually he turned to the lady on his left and said, 'That woman has talked about nothing but her insides ever since we sat down. Do you think I should charge her £100 consultation fee?'

'Certainly,' came the sympathetic reply. 'That'll be £50 – I'm a lawyer.'

ORDER IN THE COURTHOUSE

The judge glared down from his bench at the prospective juror.

'And just why is it,' he asked, 'that you don't want to serve on this jury?'

'Well, Your Honour, I'm biased. One look at that man convinced me that he is guilty.'

The judge scowled. '*That* man is not the defendant, he's the prosecuting counsel!'

JUDICIAL ORDER

The courtroom kept an anxious silence as the judge solemnly considered his verdict in the paternity suit before him.

Suddenly he reached into the fold of his robes and drew out a cigar. Ceremoniously, he handed it to the defendant.

Everyone held still.

'Congratulations!' said the judge. 'You have just become a father!'

LEGAL ORDER

'I think I'm married to a rabbit,' a woman in the USA complained to her lawyer. 'He no sooner tops me than he's through! I never get any satisfaction, and I'm quitting. I want a divorce.'

The lawyer said that before he took this case, he'd have to look up the law on the subject. 'Please return tomorrow.'

So the next day she came back.

'Madam,' said the lawyer, 'I've looked carefully at the law involved in your case, and I'm sorry to say there's nothing you can do about it. In this state, when the man is through, the woman is fucked.'

SCOTS ORDER

A wily Scot had a long-standing dispute with his neighbour. He decided to take his case to law.

He went to the most eminent lawyer in Edinburgh and for an hour explained the facts to him. When he'd finished, he said, 'Noo – tell me this. If I proceed wi' the case, hae I a chance of winning?'

'Certainly, sir. That's an excellent case you've outlined to me!'

'Then I'll take no proceeding,' said the Scot. 'That was my neighbour's case I was reciting tae ye.'

POLITICAL ORDER

Sincerity? Every politician must have sincerity. It's essential.

If you can fake that, you can fake anything.

OLD TORY TRADITION

Disraeli is said to have commented on Gladstone, 'I wish I was as sure of anything as he is of everything.'

SOUNDS RIGHT!

They say Harold Macmillan was searching for the collective name for a group of former prime ministers like himself.

He thought aloud 'A flock? As of sheep? . . . No, No!'

Then, 'A pack? As of wolves? . . . No, No!'

Then, 'Ah – I have it! A lack!'

'A lack of what?' someone asked.

'Of principles,' he said.

OLD TRADITION?

Why is the condom now a favourite topic for politicians? Because:

1 it restricts inflation
2 it provides protection for a load of pricks
3 it halts production
4 it gives a false sense of security whilst you're being screwed.

Work hard! Be faithful! You'll get your just reward.

THE LAWYER OUTWITTED

Of a rich counsellor I write,
Who had an only daughter,
Who was of youthful beauty bright,
Now mark what follows after:
Her uncle left her, I declare,
A sumptuous large possession,
Her father he was to take care,
        was to take care
        of her at his discretion.

She had ten thousand pound a year,
In gold and silver ready,
And courted was by many a Peer,
Yet none could gain this lady.
At length a squire's youngest son,
In private came a-wooing.
And when he had her favour won,
        her favour won
        he fear'd his utter ruin.

The youthful lady straightway cried,
'I must confess I love thee.
Though Lords and Knights I have denied,
Yet none I prize above thee;
Thou art a jewel in my eye,
But here,' said she, 'the care is,
I fear you will be doom'd to die
        be doom'd to die,
        For stealing of an Heiress.'

The young man he replied to her,
Like a true politician;
'Thy father is a Counsellor,
I'll tell him my condition,

Ten guineas, love, shall be his fee,
He'll think it is some stranger,
Thus for the gold, he'll counsel me,
> *he'll counsel me*
>> *and keep me safe from danger.*

Unto her father he did go
The very next day after,
But did not the lawyer know,
The lady was his daughter:
But when the lawyer saw the gold,
A pleasant trick to him he told,
> *to him he told,*
>> *with safety to obtain her.*

'Let her provide a horse,' he cried,
'And take you up behind her,
Thus with you to some parson ride
Before her parents find her;
Then she steals you, you may complain,
And so avoid the fury;
Now this is law I will maintain,
> *I will maintain,*
>> *before either Judge or jury.*

'Now take my writing and my seal
Which I cannot deny thee,
And if you any trouble feel
In court I will stand by thee.'
'I give you thanks,' the young man cried,
'By you I am befriended
And to your house I'll bring my bride,
> *I'll bring my bride,*
>> *After the work is ended.'*

Next morning by the break of day,
This news to her he carried.
He did her father's counsel take,
And they were fairly married.

When they all night had took their ease,
In joys beyond expressing,
They home return'd where on their knees,
    where on their knees,
        they ask'd their father's blessing.

Now when he had beheld them both,
He seem'd like one distracted,
And vowed to be reveng'd in wrath,
For what they then had acted,
With that bespoke his new made son,
'There can be no indicting,
That this is Law which we have done,
    which we have done,
        here is your own hand writing.'

The Counsellor did then reply,
'Was ever man so fitted?
My hand and seal I can't deny;
By you I am outwitted;
Ten thousand pounds a year in store,
She has left by my brother;
And when I die there will be more,
    there will be more,
        for child I have no other.'

'She might have had a Lord or Knight,
From royal loins descended;
But since thou art her heart's delight
I will not be offended:
If I the Gordian Knot should break,
'Twere cruel out of Measure;
Enjoy thy love with all my heart,
    with all my heart,
        in plenty, peace and pleasure.'

Clergy

LOW CHURCH

When Oliver Cromwell died, a chaplain who preached a funeral oration said that he knew the great man was in Heaven as surely as he himself could touch the head of his pulpit.

And reaching up his hand, he came short thereof by half a yard.

CAR STICKER

Help a nun kick the habit.

PRAISE

The chief of a primitive tribe wrote a letter to the head of the religious order which had sent three missionaries to them some months before.

The chief wrote: 'Reverend Sir, I would just like to thank you for sending out the missionaries to us. I and my tribe found them kind, compassionate, loving, wise, sensitive – and absolutely delicious.'

FIRST LESSONS

A visiting minister was asked to take Sunday School. He gave what he hoped was a brief and vivid explanation of Heaven and Hell.

'So now who can tell me,' he asked when he had finished, 'where little boys and girls go when they do bad things?'

Silence.

Then Willy piped up, 'Back of the churchyard.'

TAKING THE OATH

Playing golf the clergyman was digging in with his sand wedge, trying to get out of the bunker. He finally got the ball aloft only to see it roll over the green and into the bunker on the far side.

Red-faced and exasperated, he turned to the other members of the foursome and said, 'Won't one of you laymen please say a few appropriate words?'

LOST APPEAL

A middle-aged much-married Irish farm worker was taken to task by his parish priest.

'Now look here, Sean,' said the Holy Father, 'I've not objected to your four previous wives being Protestants because you've been a good son of the Church and converted them all to the one true faith. But this last wife of yours is also a Protestant; you've been married to her for two years and not once has she set foot in the confessional to ask for instruction.'

'Ah well, ye see, Father,' said Sean, 'the ould converter's not what it was.'

QUICK ANSWER

'Name one thing that's worse than drink!' yelled the evangelist.

'Thirst!' yelled a voice from the back.

GENERAL CONFESSION

In the confessional, a man says, 'Father, I've *really* sinned!'

The priest says, 'Well, my son, what's the trouble?'

'I've had sex.'

'Is there something especially wrong with that?'

Long pause.

Then the man says, 'With Jim.'

'Ah. That *is* a sin! Well, you have to say thirty-six Hail Mary's and whatever else they say. And five pounds in the Poor Plate as you go out. And come back and talk to me again.'

Another fellow comes in and says, 'Father, I've had sex. I've committed a sin.'

'With Mary?'

'No, no.'

'With whom?'

Long pause.

'With Jim?'

'Yes.'

And before the hour was out, four other men came in to confess that they'd sinned . . . 'With Jim'.

Then a sixth fellow came in. 'Father, I have sinned.'

'Don't tell me! With Jim?'

'No.'

Ah, thought the priest, at last a good old-fashioned sinner!

'I *am* Jim.'

CURATE'S EGG

Visitors dropped in on their curate just as he answered the phone. They couldn't avoid overhearing the conversation:

Female caller: 'Darling, I'm pregnant again.'

Curate: 'Yes! Who's speaking?'

LONESOME?

LIKE TO MEET PEOPLE?
LIKE A CHANGE?
LIKE EXCITEMENT?
LIKE A NEW JOB?

JUST
SCREW UP
ONE MORE
TIME!

QUICK TUMBLE

A young couple came to see the vicar to arrange to have the banns called.

The fiancé said, 'Tell me, Vicar, do you believe in sex before the wedding?'

'Not if it delays the ceremony . . .'

PARABLE OF THE SACRISTAN

Walker was illiterate, in the old days when that was fairly common. In fact, he had been sacristan at his local church for many years. But a new vicar came and a new rule was set up that illiterates could no longer serve in church positions.

And so Walker was left unemployed. He was given a small parting pay packet, and that was that.

He thought he'd ask about a job at a stationer's in his home town, but found to his surprise that there was no stationer's shop in a central location. He used his pay packet to rent a shop, worked hard and invested wisely. When he reached middle age he owned several such shops and was among the richest and most respected men in the county.

By this time, the vicar had died. But his replacement organised a service to pay tribute to Walker's achievements. It was a big occasion, and Walker was asked to say a few words.

The clergyman introduced him with a short speech, and wound up with, 'It's amazing, Mr Walker, that you have come so far without being able to read or write. Can you imagine where you would be today if you were literate?'

'Certainly,' said Walker. 'I'd be a church sacristan.'

A LITTLE BIT OFF THE TOP

When I was eight days old, my boys,
Hurrah, hurrah,
When I was eight days old, my boys,
Hurrah, hurrah,
The rabbi came with a big sharp knife,
And I surely thought he would take my life,
But all he took was a little bit off the top.

Oh, that is what they call a bris,
Hurrah, hurrah,
Oh, that is what they call a bris,
Hurrah, hurrah,
And if the rabbi doesn't miss,
It makes for a more interesting piss,
But all he took was a little bit off the top.

The rabbi, he is called a moyl,
Hurrah, hurrah,
The rabbi, he is called a moyl,
Hurrah, hurrah,
And over me he sure did toil.
If he'd cut off more, I'd have been a goil,
But all he took was a little bit off the top.

Oh circumcision is all right,
Hurrah, hurrah,
Oh circumcision is all right,
Hurrah, hurrah,
But every morning and every night,
You aim to the left and pee to the right,
But all he took was a little bit off the top.

NOT FAR-SIGHTED ENOUGH

'What is the best position for me to assume, doctor, while I'm having my baby?'

'I'd say the same as when you made the baby.'

'You mean I've got to be driven around Hyde Park in a taxi for two hours with my feet hanging out of the rear window?'

Doctors

ALL IN DUE COURSE

'Dr North!' said the theatre nurse sharply during an operation. 'You're not concentrating!'

'What do you mean, nurse?' asked the surgeon.

'You just asked for a number three iron!'

PROFESSIONAL SECRETS

When the doctor's son qualified as an MD he joined his father's practice and they agreed that the son should now make the house calls.

After three months he was accepted by the many patients he had visited – they all said that he would do very well.

'I'll tell you something, Dad,' he said one evening at supper. 'I don't want to crow, but I've finally cleared up old Mrs Curtis' back trouble.' He was obviously very pleased with his own clinical brilliance.

'Is that a fact?' remarked his father. 'Well now, that's fine, my boy, just fine. Especially as it was that back that put you through medical school.'

ON THE OTHER HAND

Winston Churchill agreed with the old saying, 'An apple a day keeps the doctor away.'

'But when should you take this apple?' he was asked.

'When the doctor arrives. And then throw it at him!'

CHRONIC PATIENT

'Doctor, I wake up laughing at myself.'

'I've told you before, Mr Horton, you should wear pyjamas!'

FAR-SIGHTED

A very eminent eye-doctor was retiring. He was presented by his colleagues with a specially commissioned portrait featuring the doctor himself in the centre of a huge eye.

'That's very fine,' he said after unveiling the painting. 'But what a good thing it was that I decided not to be a gynaecologist!'

MORE DIFFICULTIES

A woman waiting in the artificial insemination clinic was taken aback when she saw her physician enter the room and begin to remove his trousers.

'What are you doing?' she cried as his underpants came off too.

'We've run out of bottles,' he explained, 'so you'll have to have draught.'

AND MORE

Wilbur felt a cold coming on and went to a doctor. Before he could explain why he had come, the nurse sent him to the next room and told him to strip there. Another man was already there, stark naked, with his clothes in a pile on one arm and a package in the other.

'Can you imagine,' Wilbur complained to him, 'that nurse sent me in here to take off all my clothes! And I only have a sore throat!'

'That's nothing,' said the man. 'I came here to deliver a package!'

COMPLAINT

A patient known for claiming sick-leave from his job for one ailment after another called once again at the doctor's surgery. But it was a very busy morning and his turn was a long time coming.

When he finally got in, he was annoyed. 'I've been in your waiting room so long,' he said, 'I bet I've caught three more diseases!'

The doctor asked, 'Well, what's wrong this time?'

'OK, *I'll* tell *you* this time! I need something to make me sweat.'

'I agree with you,' said the doctor, as he certified him fit for work.

AND ANOTHER

'I'm not sure I'm going to come to this doctor anymore,' one patient said to another.

'Why? What has he done?'

'He's been treating a man for yellow jaundice for ten years. And he just found out the man is Chinese.'

'So what?'

'What's terrible is, he cured him!'

'Oh, that explains the difference in our salaries!'

ECHO VALLEY

'Good gracious, you've got the largest cavity I've ever seen,' the gynaecologist exclaimed as he examined a new patient. 'The largest cavity I've ever seen!'

'I heard the first time,' snapped the patient, 'you don't have to repeat yourself!'

'But I didn't,' said the doctor.

Psychiatrists

QUICK LEARNER

A psychiatrist arriving unexpectedly early at his office one morning was appalled to hear the janitor answer the phone and say, 'Yes, Miss? . . . I see . . . yes . . . yes . . . no . . . yes . . . Well, the best thing I can suggest is that you go out and get yourself screwed . . .'

SLOW LEARNER

Two men who'd been in school together happened to meet one day on the street. After greetings, etc., they had a good chat.

'Where are you working, Joe?' asked Don.

'Oh, I'm practising as a psychiatrist.'

'Never knew that was your ambition,' Don said, surprised.

'It wasn't,' Jim answered, looking very bitter. 'I wanted to be a sex maniac, but I failed the practical.'

DOUBLE LEARNER

A man rushed into a psychiatrist's consulting room, saying he thought he had a split personality.

'All right,' replied the psychiatrist. 'That will be fifty quid each.'

NOT A LEARNER

Another patient came in to tell the doctor that she still couldn't resist picking things up in shops and putting them in her pockets.

'Don't worry,' he said reassuringly. 'I've sorted out your problem. You're a thief.'

MEDICAL HELP

A beautiful girl was talking to her psychiatrist about her behaviour.

'It's liquor, doctor. Whenever I have a few drinks I have a compulsion to make love to whomever I happen to be with at the time.'

'I see,' said the doctor. 'Well, suppose I just mix us a couple of cocktails, then you and I sit down nice and relaxed and discuss this compulsive neurosis of yours.'

Dentists

NOT MEDICAL HELP

A man who had no teeth had to share his table in a restaurant with a stranger. The stranger noticed that the man was finding it difficult to chew.

'Excuse me, but I may be able to help,' he said, and he took some false teeth out of his pocket and politely offered them. The man was grateful, but the teeth were too loose.

The stranger then offered another set, but these were too tight.

A third set, however, were a perfect fit.

'Thank you so much, thank you, thank you!' said the man, 'What a piece of luck for me to share my table with a fine dentist!'

'Dentist? What do you mean, dentist?' said the stranger. 'I'm an undertaker.'

ALF GARNETT TOLD THIS ONE

The dentist said, 'I'm sorry to have to tell you that you need a complete dental job, wisdom tooth to wisdom tooth and top to bottom! It will cost you £2,000.'

Cohen said, '*You're* sorry? *I'm* sorry I have to tell you that I can't afford that much! Look, I've been coming to you for years. Is there any way you can make the price more reasonable?'

'No, I can't, but I can recommend a younger man. He might do it.'

Cohen went to the younger man. The young dentist said he was trying to get established but he'd done this sort of job some time ago, on a Mr Levy.

'I'll give you his phone number,' he said. 'You can talk to him, and if you're satisfied with what he says, then come and talk to me again.'

So Cohen phoned Levy.

'Ah yes,' said Levy, 'my teeth. Well, the dentist did the work some time ago. About two years later I went to visit my daughter in Florida. Florida! She's married to a very wealthy man, you can imagine! They were in a swank hotel with all the comforts and plenty to drink, and I had a room of my own, and I swam in the hotel pool every day. Had it all to myself! Used to swim bare, how's that for privileges?'

'That's fine, Mr Levy, but how about your teeth?'

'I'm telling you; you asked me, and I'm telling you!'

He continued. 'One day when I was in the pool a beautiful young lady dived in, and she had no clothes on, neither! She swam up close to me. I was so embarrassed I didn't know what to do. But she smiled in the friendliest way and came closer and closer. Then she put her hand on me!'

'And?'

'And for the first time in two years my teeth stopped hurting!'

The Office

BEAUTY CONTEST

One of the firm's management experts stopped to speak to a glamorous secretary.

'I'm bound to tell you that I shall put in my report that you waste too much time on your appearance.'

'Go ahead,' she said, 'but I've only been here two months and I've just got engaged to the boss, so it hasn't been entirely wasted.'

ALL YOU NEED TO KNOW ABOUT COMPUTERS

Computers are almost human. One even had a screw loose.

A giant computer was installed in London by the army. An officer asked it, 'How far is it from A to B?'

The computer replied, 'Six thousand.'

The officer then fed in the question, 'Six thousand what?'

And the computer replied, 'Six thousand, sir!'

The electronic computer saves man a lot of guesswork – but so does a bikini.

MOTHER-IN-LAW

The President of the company apologized to his Board of Directors that he had to leave in the middle of a meeting.

'You know how it is, boys. My mother-in-law is arriving on the five o'clock broom.'

UPTOWN

The new young man in the office left work late one evening and walked down his usual street to the bus stop. It was now quite dark.

A girl appeared. 'Come with me for a quickie?' she asked.

He didn't know what a quickie was. 'N-no. No, no,' he replied.

'Only ten pounds?'

'No, no.'

A short time later another female approached him.

'Ten pounds for a quickie?' she asked.

'No, no!'

The next morning in the office he asked the head typist, 'What's a quickie?'

'You mean you want one?' she smiled. 'Didn't think you'd be interested. It's ten pounds, same as downtown.'

DOWNTOWN

Overheard in an office, from a businessman to a client: 'I would describe your financial situation as fluid. Which is a nice way of saying you're going down the drain.'

MIDTOWN

A gentleman collecting for charity had come to visit Mr Moneybags at his office.

He said, 'Mr Moneybags, we have frequently tried to solicit funds for our worthy charity from you and you have never responded. This has seemed odd to us and we have checked up on you. We find you not only have an elaborate town house in London, but you also have a country home in Sussex. You have three Rolls Royces, belong to two expensive clubs, and of course you have your thriving chain of department stores in a dozen big cities. How can you refuse a contribution to our cause in view of your great wealth?'

Mr Moneybags considered, then said, 'Actually, I also have a place in France which you seem to have overlooked, and my chain of stores extends to five countries. However, have you any idea of the situation in my family? Did you, by any chance, learn that my mother has a heart condition that demands continual private hospital care – with prices the way they are now? Do you know I have three sisters with three sons each, all of whom are at fancy schools – and do you know the cost of tuition? Do you know how much it takes to educate them? I don't give any of *them* a brass farthing, so why should I give anything to you? Go elsewhere with your requests!'

HOMEWORK

The elderly boss, with a well-earned reputation for being a bit of a lad, phoned his wife one evening soon after seven o'clock.

'I'll have to skip dinner again, darling,' he told her. 'I'm working on something very important.'

'Why don't you bring the work home with you,' suggested his wife, 'I'd like to meet her too.'

OFFICE MERRY-GO-ROUND

A businessman whose wife was running around with other men decided to bring matters to a head. He wrote the following letter to Mr Brown.

Dear Sir,
I am fully aware of your relations with my wife. Be at my office at two o'clock sharp on Monday.
Yours truly,
H. Higgins.

Brown, when he received the letter, called in his secretary. 'Susie,' he said, 'take this down:'

My dear Higgins,
Your circular letter received. Will attend conference on time.

MAFIACO
INCORPORATED
FINANCIAL STATEMENT – FISCAL YEAR 1988

INCOME BEFORE TAXES	$ 12,789,568,598.04
INCOME AFTER TAXES	12,789,568,598.04
ADJUSTED NET INCOME	12,789,568,598.04

ASSETS

Cash and Securities

Buried in cellars, etc	$ 47,368,537,907.98
Deposited in Swiss Bank Accounts, etc.	8,638,209,488.11
Invested in Sicilian Savings Bonds	700,000,000.00
Stashed in Bus and Railroad Terminal Lockers	3,860,389,680.67

Accounts Receivable

Short Term Notes	126,578,790.50
Interest Due On Short Term Notes	29,589,477,202.29

Inventories

Contracts and Work in Progress	589,700,000.00

Equipment

Bullet-Proof Cadillacs and Lincolns	2,863,985.17
Tanks and Armored Cars, etc	1,685,300.54
Guns and Ammunition	58,806,276.49
Brass Knuckles, Black Jacks and Other Weapons	388,974.39
	90,936,637,655.14

Less Depreciation for Obsolescence

(238,589 Double-Breasted Striped Suits)	417,685.25
	90,936,219,969.89

Properties and Other Interests

Las Vegas	127,568,778,622.03
Miami Beach	70,433,889,457.86
Monaco	1,687,742.59
Benidorm	980,066.23
Cannes	6,299,754.01
Salerno (122,689,500,000 lire)	1,022.00
TOTAL ASSETS	**$288,947,856,634.61**

LIABILITIES

Wages and Salaries

Executives	150,000,000,000.00
Executives' Wives	81,000,000,000.00
Executives' Relatives	47,000,000,000.00
Executives' Relatives' Wives	9,000,000,000.00
Employees	890,000.00

Expenses

Payoffs To Law Enforcement Officers	927,908,567.00
Payoffs To Government Officials and Judges	69,865,427.00
Funeral Costs	12,680,287.21
Dental Bills For Show Biz Personalities We Own	72,684.00
Auditors Fees*	439,669.40
TOTAL LIABILITIES	**$288,947,856,634.61**

AUDITOR'S REPORT TO STOCKHOLDERS

* We have examined the books and financial statements of MAFIACO and in our opinion it represents fairly the results of its operations and the financial position of MAFIACO for the fiscal year of 1988, and anybody don't like it gets his.

(signed) Alfonso "Big Fish" Baccala

OFFICE INCENTIVES

The owner of a large firm bought a number of signs reading DO IT NOW! and hung them in prominent places around his office, hoping to inspire promptness and energy.

Several days later a friend asked him how the scheme had affected the staff.

'Well, not the way I thought,' the businessman answered. 'The cashier ran off with £15,000, the head bookkeeper eloped with my private secretary, and three clerks asked for a rise.'

NAKED AMBITION

'When I got back to my office my secretary told me she had a new position.'

'What did you say?'

'I said, "Shut the door and let's try it".'

INTERNATIONAL DIFFERENCES?

Edwina Currie's statement that businessmen should bring their wives with them when they travel runs counter to the respected traditions of American corporations.

A favourite song used to be an oldie set to a catchy tune, called 'There Ain't No Flies on Us'. But at today's deluxe conferences at deluxe resorts, it goes:

There ain't no wives with us,
There ain't no wives with us.
There may be wives with some of you guys,
But there ain't no wives with us.

VERBAL HARRASSMENT

One secretary met another on the street.

'Why, hello, Phyllis! I thought you were working for that handsome wealthy tycoon.'

'Oh, I was. But I had to give notice when I realized he was interested in only one thing.'

'Eh?'

'How many words per minute.'

EXECUTIVE DRESS

'Don't you think he dresses nattily?' one secretary asked another as they walked past a young executive.

'Natalie who?'

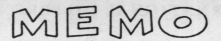

MEMO

IN REGARDS TO YOUR
RECENT MEMO

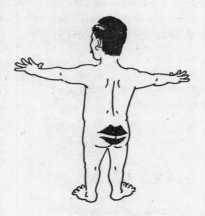

THE PERFECT SECRETARY

Happy wife to a circle of friends:
'Jeff's new secretary has everything – no looks, no figure, no personality!'

Veterinaries

A WAY TO STOP IT

After complaints from the neighbours, Harry had sadly agreed to have a vet make his cat fit to guard a sultan's harem.

'I'll bet,' said one neighbour, 'that that ex-tom of yours just lies on the hearth now and gets fat.'

'No, he still goes out at night. But now he goes along as a consultant.'

ANOTHER WAY

At three o'clock in the morning, old Mrs Eddy phoned the vet.

'I'm sorry to disturb you,' she began, 'but my pussycat, Arthur, is outside with a girl pussycat from next door, and they are – well, you know . . .'

'Mating, Mrs Eddy?'

'Er – Yes. But the point is that they've been doing it for hours now! They're making awful noises. I don't know how to stop them. What can I do?'

'Pick Arthur up and bring him to the phone.'

'Bring him to the phone? Will that stop him?'

'It stopped me, Mrs Eddy . . .'

Other Occupations

GENEALOGIST

A man who will trace your family tree as far back as your money will go.

TEACHING

Universities have devised a comprehensive final exam that covers all subjects:

Question 1. History. Describe the history of the papacy, showing its social, political and economic impact on the world. You have ten minutes.

Question 2. Biology. Create life. You have five minutes.

Question 3. Medicine. Remove your appendix. You have fifteen minutes.

Question 4. Political Science. On the desk next to you is a red telephone. Take it up and start World War III.

GOLF PRO

A new member at the club hit a drive from the first tee that was the longest ever seen at the course, but it was completely in the wrong direction. Out of bounds, over a high fence, no chance of playing it. So the man took another ball, made another drive and went on to play the eighteen holes.

He was in the clubhouse, and had had a couple of drinks when the club professional came over.

'Excuse me, sir. Are you the gentleman who hit that amazing drive off the first tee?'

'That's me. Damn good drive I thought, don't you agree?'

The pro just shook his head sadly. 'Very long drive, no doubt of that. But I'm sorry to say there have been some unfortunate results.'

'What do you mean?'

'Well,' said the pro, 'the ball went over the fence which runs along the main road. It hit a motorcyclist and killed him instantly. The motorbike crashed into a car, and the car crossed the central barrier and collided at eighty miles an hour with a coach full of old folks from the Darby and Joan Club. The coach ran into a minibus which smashed into a double-decker. The bus ripped off the road and ploughed through the wall of an orphanage. The latest report is forty-seven dead and sixty injured.'

The man looked at him in horror. 'Oh my God,' he cried, 'this is awful! It's terrible! What should I do?'

'Well, sir,' replied the pro, 'if I were you, next time try a different grip, keep your weight over the ball, try not to pull on your follow-through . . .'

SAILORS

One foggy night at sea the captain of a ship saw what looked like the lights of another ship heading directly towards him. He signalled the other ship: 'Change your course ten degrees starboard.'

The reply came back: 'Change your course ten degrees port.'

The captain answered: 'I am a captain. Change YOUR course ten degrees starboard.'

The reply came: 'I am a seaman first class – change YOUR course ten degrees port.'

By now the captain was really angry, so he signalled back: 'I am a US battleship – change YOUR course ten degrees starboard.'

Reply: 'I am a lighthouse. Change YOUR course ten degrees port.'

A Navy ship had a day's leave at a Pacific island famed for its beautiful native girls. One sailor quickly got busy placing groups of them to advantage and photographing them.

An officer watched him for some time and then asked, 'Where do you think you're going to get all those films developed?'

The sailor asked, 'Films? Who's got films?'

'System been down long?'

REPAIR MEN

The caretaker of a twelve-storey building was told that a lift had got jammed between two floors with a passenger inside. He pushed his way through the crowd to the lift shaft. 'Don't worry,' he called to the trapped passenger. 'We'll soon have you out. I've sent for a lift repair man.'

A tense voice called back: 'I am the lift repair man!'

A handsome young gasman from Chester
Grabbed hold of a blonde and undressed her.
Said he, 'This is sweeter
Than reading your meter.'
And they then took a lengthy siesta.

A plumber was summoned to a mansion to fix a leak, and tried his luck with a pretty maid. She refused on the grounds that her mistress was at home and she didn't want to get fired.

Next morning she called him to say that her mistress was out, and would he like to come over and see her?

'What!' yelled the plumber. 'On my own time?'

MUSICIANS

An orchestra was scheduled for a concert with a chorus made up of several church choirs, all of whom had been practising their parts separately for almost the whole year.

At rehearsal, the conductor had a difficult job to get things as he wanted. Despite differences in their preparations, the singer and the musicians would have to work as an ensemble.

The conductor tried several times. Then in the middle of a phrase he put his baton down. The orchestra knew *something* was to come.

What he said was: 'If the ladies will look down at their parts, they will see where the gentlemen enter.'

On another occasion a new musician arrived late, and the rehearsal had already begun.

The annoyed conductor asked, 'What is your name, sir?'

'Ball, sir.'

'How very singular . . .'

A conductor became increasingly annoyed at the incompetence of a lady cellist.

'You don't seem to realize that between your legs is a wonderful instrument! And all you do is sit there and scratch it!'

FROM YORKSHIRE MINERS

When the management was at the height of increasing productivity, ending piece-work and establishing new shift patterns, a West Riding collier was called in to account for his persistent absenteeism.

'Why,' asked the manager, 'do you work only four shifts?'

'Because,' replied the collier, 'I can't get by on only three.'

Derbyshire dumplings born and bred,
Are strong i' the arm and weak i' the head.

Him? He ain't a Black, he's a smoked Irishman.

MANUFACTURERS

Messrs Bristle & Bucket, a building materials shop, wrote
to their paint stockist:

*We complained to you several weeks ago about the distemper we
purchased from you. Please arrange to collect the paint.*

Paint stockist to distemper manufacturer:

*One of our best customers has complained about your distemper and
returned it. Please arrange to pick up our entire stock and pass
credit.*

Distemper manufacturer to paint stockist:

*We regret the tone of your letter and are not prepared to take back the
material. However, our technical representative will call in due
course.*

Paint stockist to distemper manufacturer:

*With reference to the visit of your technical representative, please
confirm in writing that we can sell the distemper as a knifing
filler.*

Director, distemper manufacturer, to sales manager:

*You were right to refuse to take back the distemper, but I doubt the
wisdom of sending our technical representative. Write to our stockist
to sell his stocks of distemper as a ready-for-use filler.*
P.S. Fire the technical representative.

Paint stockist to distemper manufacturer:

*Orders are piling up for your ready-for-use filler. Please rush through
100 × 4 lb tins.*

Director, distemper manufacturer, to sales manager:

*The Board has decided to enter the filler market. Arrangements have
been made for an all-out advertising campaign in the press and
television. Please issue a sales bulletin listing the advantages of our*

filler – easily applied, fine texture, dries quickly, easy to rub down. Mention that it is the only filler on the market available in twenty-four colours.

Director, distemper manufacturer, to sales manager:

Arrangements for our ready-to-use filler convention at the Grand Hotel are complete. Five hundred of our best customers and the press are coming, and the President of the Master Decorators Association will take the chair.

Sales manager, distemper manufacturer, to Mr G. Bristle of Messrs Bristle & Bucket:

As a leading user of our ready-to-use filler, we wonder whether you would do us the honour of being a guest at our convention at the Grand Hotel.

Mr G. Bristle to sales manager, distemper manufacturer:

Thank you for your kind invitation. I shall be delighted to attend. As you know, we have purchased a great deal of this material in the past few months, and would mention in passing that when thinned down with water it makes a really excellent washable distemper . . .

Ethnics and Nationals

DON'T BE ETHNIC!

An Italian, a Jew and a Greek were walking along a beach when they found an old bronze lamp. Out of curiosity they picked it up and rubbed it off.

A huge swirl of mist came out of it – and turned into a genie!

The genie said, 'I'm going to grant each of you a wish, but it's on one condition only. You can't do anything ethnic for twenty-four hours. If you do, you'll vanish!'

The three men continued walking, marvelling at their good fortune. They passed a restaurant from which came the delicious smell of lasagne and pasta and spaghetti. The Italian sniffed with pleasure and said, 'I'm hungry. I'm going to go in and eat.'

'Oh, no, you can't!' said the Greek and the Jew. 'Don't do it. For you, that's ethnic!'

The Italian said, 'You're being ridiculous. Everybody's got to eat.'

So he went in, but as he stepped through the door – poof! – he vanished.

The Jew and the Greek shook their heads and walked on.

Down the street they saw a five-pound note lying on the footpath. The Jew said, 'Look, somebody dropped that money. I'm going to pick it up.'

'No!' cried the Greek. 'You can't do that! That's ethnic!'

'Nonsense,' said the Jew. 'Everybody needs money.' And he bent over to pick it up.

Poof! – both the Jew and the Greek vanished.

ETHNIC SINS?

During World War II three chaplains were quartered together, and when they had the time they had occasional theological discussions. Just before D-Day they talked about death, which now seemed a likely possibility.

'Death makes you realize the importance of unburdening your soul,' said the Irish Catholic chaplain. 'I must confess I have a terrible impulse to drink. I fight it, oh, I fight it! But every once in a while, I fall!'

'Well,' said the Anglican chaplain. 'I don't have too much trouble with liquor, but – I have a dangerous impulse towards women. I fight it desperately, but every once in a while I'm tempted – and fall.'

After that there was a pause. Then they turned to the Jewish chaplain. One of them asked him, 'How about you, Chaplain Levy, are you burdened with a besetting sin, too?'

The Jewish chaplain sighed. 'I'm afraid so. I have this terrible, irresistible impulse to gossip.'

ETHNIC PROTEST

A West Indian objected to books in the local library which contained the word 'nigger'.

The prim white librarian refused to withdraw the books. She pointed out that other offensive words like 'bastard' appear in books too.

'Yes,' said the West Indian, 'but us niggers is organized and you bastards ain't.'

ETHNIC VISION

Groom: 'My darling! I've a confession to make. I'm colour-blind.
Bride: 'Yo' sho am, honey! Yo' sho am!'

IMMIGRATION MIX-UP

A Pakistani illegal immigrant thought he could be naturalized if he became Irish. So he visited a brain surgeon, who told him he'd need to have three-quarters of his brain removed in order to become an Irishman.

The Pakistani said, 'Very good. I pay. You fix me up.'

However, the doctor made a mistake and removed five-sixths of his brain.

When the Pakistani woke up, the surgeon tried to tell him what had happened. The Pakistani sat up in bed and said: 'That's perfectly all right, old chap. I don't mind being English.'

AUSSIES

What's the difference between an Australian wedding and an Australian funeral?

There's one less drunk at the funeral.

WANT TO LEARN AUSTRALIAN?

An Aussie in a cozzie who doesn't know the meaning of a hizzie in a hozzie might feel out of place at a wharfie's picnic.

(A wharfie is a docker, a hizzie is a hysterectomy, a hozzie is a hospital, a cozzie is a swimsuit.)

The average truckie, taking a perve, with a verandah over his toy shop, is as happy as a bastard on Father's Day.

(A truckie is a lorry driver, to perve is to gaze lustfully, the verandah in question is a paunch.)

IRISH AGAIN

What about the Irish night-club that employed a chucker-in?

AMERICANS

The French used to make fun of the 'melting-pot' USA. They said that whenever an American had nothing to do, he could amuse himself trying to find out who his grandfather was.

The Americans retorted, 'And whenever a Frenchman has nothing to do, he can amuse himself trying to find out who his father was.'

INTERNATIONAL POLITICS

Mitterand, Gorbachov and Maggie Thatcher were watching television at a Summit conference, but the sound was off, and they began to argue about whom they were watching.

Mitterand: 'See how they share everything and settle differences by discussion. They're Socialists!'

Gorbachov: 'No! See how they agree and obey, and consequently how peaceful they are. They're Russians!'

Maggie: 'Never! They have nothing to wear, they have no work to do, they have nowhere to go, and they have almost nothing to eat, and then they think they're better off than anyone else. They're English!'

CUT YOUR LOSSES, MY BOY

Two Jewish businessmen met on Finchley Road, London.

'So what's new?'

'I'm married now.'

'Well, how nice! Congratulations!'

'Who is she?'

'Oh, you don't know her – she was Maureeen Kelly.'

'You mean to say you married a goy!'

'Yeah, I married a goy. Believe me, it's much better!'

'What do you mean, better? You should've married a nice Jewish girl like everyone else!'

'Oh yeah? So if I married a nice Jewish girl, first I'd have to give her an engagement diamond as big as the Ritz. Then I'd have to pay for a big party at a big hotel bigger than the Ritz! The more I'd pay the more she could crow over her friends. I'd have to give a bachelor dinner for all her male relatives. I'd have to pay money down for a big flat in Golders Green, and pay money down for the mortgage, and money down for the furniture! Then I'd have to take her on a honeymoon to Miami, no less, and buy her new clothes for the climate, new beach sandals, £100 a pair they cost! And when we got back to London she'd announce she had to have a full-time maid and full-time cook. Next she'd say we had to give a big dinner party. But would it be to use the maid and the cook? Not on your life! It would be in the most expensive restaurant in London. Next she'd want a Christmas holiday, ski-ing, and all the clothes for that. Then she'd have to go to theatres and nightclubs, every night of the week! After all that, she wouldn't feel so good, she'd have a headache. So she'd have to go to her doctor, and he would send her to a specialist – for headache! A week later she'd have to go to her doctor again, and he'd send her to a specialist doctor for her stomach. Then she'd feel unhappy, and she'd go to her doctor again. This time he'd send her to a psychiatrist, so this psychiatrist would see her every week, and charge more than the travel companies and restaurants combined! That's how it would go!'

'But,' says the friend, 'if you marry a goy, isn't it the same?'

'If it's a goy, who cares?'

POLITICAL VIEWS

In Germany, ALL IS PROHIBITED! (except what is permitted).
In France, ALL is permitted, except what is prohibited.
In Russia, ALL IS PROHIBITED, INCLUDING WHAT IS PERMITTED!
In Italy, All is permitted; even what is prohibited is permitted.
In the UK, Much is prohibited, but no one knows what it is.

FROM POLAND

'When I came home from the factory last night, I found my wife in bed with another man. How can I prevent that happening again?'

'Work more overtime.'

In Poland a customer asks the butcher first for pork, then for lamb and lastly for beef. No luck.

When he leaves, the butcher turns to his assistant and says, 'What a fantastic memory!'

FROM RUSSIA

In the USSR, one Russian asked another, 'Is it true that Americans have more cars than we have in Russia?'

Said his friend, 'Basically, yes. But we've got much more parking space.'

'What's hot and boneless and glows in the dark?'
'Chicken Kiev.'

FROM GERMANY

Nazi stormtroopers were sent to a German café to heckle its star.

'Jewboy!' they shouted.

He smiled disarmingly. 'You are mistaken. I only look so intelligent!'

FROM ISRAEL

Did you hear about the Irishman in Israel who was living the life of Cohen?

FROM CZECHOSLOVAKIA

In a Prague café a citizen is reading a motoring magazine. Another man sits down next to him and notices that the reader is studying the pictures of a Rolls Royce and of a Russian Moskvitch car.

'I wonder which of them you'd like to have,' he says.

The man looks up and replies, 'The Moskvitch, of course.'

'Come, come! You obviously know nothing about cars!'

'Oh yes,' says the reader. 'I know a lot about cars. But I know nothing about you.'

FROM SOUTH AMERICA

There are seventy stanzas in the Uruguayan national anthem, a fact which may account for the Uruguay standing army.

SIXTEENTH-CENTURY FASHIONS

The Spaniard loves his ancient slop,
The Lombard his Venetian.
And some like breechless women go,
The Russe, Turk, Jew, and Grecian.
The thrifty Frenchman wears small waist,
The Dutch his belly boasteth,
The Englishman is for them all
And with each fashion coasteth.

IRISH FASHIONS

What is a social climber? A Kerryman with a Cork accent.

An Englishman, a Scotsman and an Irishman were captured during the French Revolution and sentenced to be hanged. No gallows was handy, so each was given his choice of tree. The Englishman chose an oak, and the Scotsman a pine. The Irishman said he would like a gooseberry tree.

The judge replied, 'A gooseberry tree is too small.'

'That's all right,' said the Irishman. 'I'll wait for it to grow.'

Another Irishman applied for a job on a building site. The foreman said 'You Paddies are an ignorant lot, so I'm going to ask you some questions to see how much you understand. Now, what's the difference between a girder and a joist?'

'Ah, that's easy,' said the Irishman. 'Girder wrote *Faust* and Joist wrote *Ulysses*.'

USA FASHIONS

In the old days, a woman killed her husband with an axe and the jury sent her to prison. She was kind of worried at first, but the work they gave her was a lot easier than what she'd had to do at home. The food was better too, and she had a good bed without bugs in it.

After two weeks she said, 'Lordy, if I had of knowed the jail-house was like this, I'd have killed that son-of-a-bitch ten years ago!'

In the south, three black boys were comparing names. The first one said, 'Ma name am Fluorescent.'

'Fluorescent?' asked the others.

'Yup, because ma Dad done invented the fluorescent light.'

The second boy said, 'Ma name am Victrola, 'cos ma Dad done invented it.'

The third said, 'Ma name am Gonorrhea.'

'Yo not sayin' yo Dad done invented that?'

'No, but he am the southern distributor.'

In The City

DRIVING

Contrary to public opinion, it's not easy to get a parking ticket in London these days.

First of all, you have to find a place to park.

For example . . .
Motoring from Birmingham, a couple finally reached their destination, London.

The husband who was driving said with relief, 'Well, we're halfway there!'

'Half!' cried the wife. 'What do you mean? The building we're heading for is right in front of us! You can see it!'

'The other half,' he continued, 'is finding a parking place.'

WALKING

Poodle in the park: 'Do you have a family tree?'
Terrier: 'No, we ain't particular.'

BY TRAIN

Station announcement in Liverpool Street: 'The train arriving on platforms 1, 2, 3, 4 and 5 is coming in sideways.'

WORKING

Shop steward: 'I vote that we only work on Tuesdays.'
Union members: 'What – *every* Tuesday?'

PHONING

Somewhere in London a man was making an obscene phone call.

'I'll be coming up to your flat tonight when your husband's out, and I'll be taking off all your clothes, and then I'll – *Will you stop telling me the time when I'm talking to you!*'

BY BUS

A man on a crowded London bus had his small son sitting on his knees.

At Marble Arch, a very pretty girl got on and stood holding a strap just in front of them.

Glancing at her, the man said, 'Get up, Johnny – and give this young lady your seat.'

ON THE STREET

A policeman on the beat stopped a woman with her breasts hanging out.

'What are you up to now, Betty? You with your blouse open making a display of yourself!'

'Don't tell me I left the bleeding baby on the bus!'

OH!

A couple were drinking pretty heavily at a night club. In fact, the man slipped under the table.

A man nearby said to the girl, 'Lady, your husband just slid under the table!'

'Oh no,' she replied, 'he couldn't have! My husband just walked in.'

CHAMBER-MADE

A chambermaid in one of London's best hotels answered a ring to the tenth floor.

The moment she entered the room, the guest seized her, threw her on the bed, and did his will. Then he ushered her to the door and pushed her out.

'To this day,' she told a friend, 'I don't know what he was ringing for!'

**Make
someone
happy!**

STOP USING THE BLOODY 'PHONE!!

MAKING THE HEADLINES

Newspaper-seller outside Bond Street station: 'Paper!
Paper! Big hoax in London's West End! Fifty victims!'

Passer-by: 'I'll have a paper – here's the 25p.' Then he
reads.

'Hey,' he cries. 'Wait a minute! There's nothing here
about a hoax.'

Newspaper-seller: 'Paper! Paper! Big hoax in London's
West End! Fifty-one victims!'

UPPER CRUST

A member of a London Club met a fellow member by chance while strolling in Hyde Park. Noticing that his friend had a handsome dog with him, he said, 'You've got a new dog.'

'Yes,' replied the other. 'I got him for my wife, as a matter of fact.'

'By Jove!' said the first. 'That was a damned good swop.'

VERY UPPER

A scientist invented a special powder that could bring stone objects to life.

Late one night he tried it out on the statue of Admiral Nelson on top of the famous pillar in Trafalgar Square. As Nelson climbed down from his pedestal, the scientist said, 'Now that you are alive, your Lordship, what is the first thing you plan to do?'

'First of all,' said Nelson grimly, drawing his sword, 'I'm going to kill every damn pigeon I can lay my hands on!'

THE PHONE RINGS

A woman answers, 'Hello?'

A male voice whispers, 'I want to touch you, I want to kiss you, I want to embrace you –'

The woman interrupts, 'All this you can tell from "Hello"?'

NOW

Your Town Can
Have a
"Professional Riot!"
No More "AMATEUR" Demonstrations

DEMONSTRATORS, INC.
"Our Trained Terrorists Can Tie Up Any Town!"

Name Your Cause — We Will Demonstrate
90 Days Advance Notice Needed to
Guarantee Spontaneity

OUR BANNER PAINTERS CAN MISSPELL ANYTHING . . . .
OUR CHANTS ARE WRITTEN SPECIALLY FOR ANY OCCASION . . . .
SPECIAL BUS RATES TO WASHINGTON D.C. . . .
OUR TRAINED CATS GUARANTEED TO DECOY POLICE DOGS . . . .
OUR PRINTERS CAN FORGE MEMBERSHIP CARDS IN ANY
ORGANIZATION.

WE SPECIALIZE IN HAND-PICKED HOODLUMS THAT CAN'T
SPEAK ENGLISH . . . ALL HAVE PASSED THE "GO LIMP" TEST!

EVERYBODY'S FIGHTING SOMETHING . . . WHY AREN'T YOU? . . . WE GUARANTEE
TO CONFUSE THE ISSUE SO NOBODY CAN ARRIVE AT A SOLUTION!

Organized Confusion is Best!

GRAFFITI

On signboards:
We should eliminate doubt, I think.

EVERY DOGMA HAS ITS DAY:

Dogma's man's best friend
Fighting like cats and dogmas
Waiting for Godogma

Michaelangelo did it lying down.
  The Pope doesn't do it.
  Professors do it with class.

There was a young lady of Exeter
So pretty that men craned their necks at her.
And one made so brave
As to violently wave
The distinguishing mark of his sex at her.

Sign in music-shop window:
Gone Chopin –
Be Bach in a minute.

Sign in a bar:
REAL EARTH-MOVING DRINKS!
  From our Figaro Cocktails
    Today's Special
    (1) Orgasm
    (2) Zombie

Signs on the road:
WARNING: Radiation area! Pre-faded genes only.

Official sign says SAVE WATER –
  Hand-painted below: DILUTE IT!

On a bumper sticker:
  I.O., I.O., as off to work I go.

More signs:
At a riot:
Gentlemen! Gentlemen! Disorder, please, disorder!

During a strike:
Sympathetic workers will not cross a picnic line.

Did you hear about . . .
The recent cigarette study that disclosed that 90% of the men who have tried Camels have gone back to women?

In The Country

HE DONE THE RIGHT THING

One time there was a country boy come to a place where they don't allow no square dancing, and everybody was doing round dances. He didn't know any of the girls, but there was a good-looking woman sitting on a bench, so he asked her to dance with him.

But she says no.

The country boy was not used to women acting like that, so he says, 'Well, you can kiss my ass!'

The woman told her husband what the country boy said, and he came out on the porch. 'You go back in there and apologize to my wife,' says he. 'Otherwise I will beat the living shit out of you!'

The country boy seen he didn't have no chance, because the woman's husband was a great big man.

So he went back in the room where they was having the dance.

'Ma'm,' says he, 'you don't need to kiss my ass, after all. Me and your husband have made other arrangements.'

SO DID NEWSPAPERS

The newspaper in a small town published in headlines *Half the Council Are Crooks*. The staff were told they'd have to retract it.

The following week a new headline ran: *Half the Council Are Not Crooks*!

IN THE WILD WEST

A cowboy riding on a lonely trail heard cries for help coming from an old farmhouse. He rode over, tied his horse to a stake and entered.

There on the bed was a naked girl, each limb tied to a different bedpost. She said faintly, 'Help me, please. Two men came here, knocked my husband unconscious and then tied me to the bed. They raped me in turn; then they left me here and carried my husband away. Please, oh please, help!'

The cowboy thought for a moment, then began taking his clothes off. 'Ma'am,' he said, 'I guess this ain't your lucky day.'

RULES OF THE HOUSE

1 Don't shoot the pianist; he's doing his damndest.
2 Please don't swear, damn you!
3 Beds 50p., with sheets, 75p.
4 No horses above the first floor.
5 No more than five in a bed.
6 Warmth provided by horse blankets, liquor and Christian zeal.
7 Funerals on the house.

WIVES

In the back country of the USA, a man named Alonzo Blake was elected Justice of the Peace.

When Squire Blake came home with the news, his whole family was mighty happy. One of the little boys said to his mother, 'Maw, are we all squires now?'

The old lady just looked at him. 'No, you fool,' she said, 'just me and your Paw.'

FILL, BOWL, FILL

One time there was a king and he had a daughter. The hired man's name was Jimmy, and he got to sparking the king's daughter, till the king seen he would have to do something about it.

The king had a pet rabbit that always come to the king's house at night, so he says if Jimmy took the rabbit and kept it for a week he could marry the king's daughter. Jimmy took it over to where he lived, and trained it so it would come when he rung a bell.

The king told his pretty servant girl, if she would fetch the rabbit he'd give her five pounds. Jimmy got the best of her, and she give him half the money besides. She picked up the rabbit and started off, but Jimmy rung the bell and the rabbit broke loose and come back. So she went home and told the king she couldn't get the rabbit.

Well, the king told his daughter if she would fetch the rabbit he'd give her two hundred pounds. The king's daughter went over and says to Jimmy, 'We are going to get married anyhow, and two hundred pounds would be nice for us to have.'

Jimmy got the best of her too, and she give him half the money besides. She picked up the rabbit and started off, but Jimmy rung the bell and the rabbit broke loose and come back. So she went home and told the king she couldn't get the rabbit.

Next the king told his wife, if she would fetch the rabbit he'd give her three hundred pounds. The king's wife done her damnedest, but Jimmy got the best of her too, and she give him half the money besides. She picked up the rabbit and started off, but Jimmy rung the bell and the rabbit broke loose and come back. So she went home and told the king she couldn't get the rabbit.

Late in the night, here comes the king himself. He says he would give five hundred pounds for the rabbit, but

Jimmy got the best of him too, and the king give him half the money besides. Then he picked up the rabbit, and he told Jimmy to come along.

When they got to the king's house there was a great big bowl sitting in the middle of the floor. The king says, 'Jimmy, are you a good singer?'

Jimmy allowed he was pretty good.

'Well, we'll call in all the people to watch, and if you can sing that bowl full, you can marry my daughter,' says the king. 'But if you don't sing it full, I am going to cut your head off.'

So Jimmy done the best he could, and this is what he sung:

The first come over was the king's own servant,
To steal away my skill.
I laid her down and honed her off,
Fill, bowl, fill!
The next come over was the king's own daughter,
To steal away my skill.
I laid her down and honed her off,
Fill, bowl, fill!
The next come over was the king's own wife,
To steal away my skill.
I laid her down and honed her off,
Fill, bowl, fill!
The last come over was the king himself,
To steal away my skill.
I –

'Hold on, Jimmy,' says the king, 'that's enough. Don't sing another word! The bowl's plum full, and you can have my daughter!'

SEEING THE COUNTRY

In his day, Mark Twain travelled over 60,000 miles by rail and never had an accident. There were 845 railroads then in the USA. In one year, deaths were reported in the newspapers as totalling 325 people. In the same year, a million were reported to have died naturally in bed.

Mark Twain concluded: 'You will excuse me for taking any more chances on those beds. The railroads are good enough for me.'

THE LAZY FARMER

Isham Byrd wouldn't do no work at all mostly, because he argued that there is a time for everything under the sun and unto each a season thereof, which is in the Bible. 'Work is a good thing in its place,' says he, 'but this here toiling between meals ain't healthy.'

The neighbours were going to bury Ish, just to keep him from starving to death. They put him in a coffin and started for the graveyard.

A stranger came along. 'Good Lord, gentlemen,' says he. 'You can't bury this man when he ain't dead! Before I'll see a man buried alive I will give him a whole wagon-load of corn!'

Ish raised his head out of the coffin. 'Stranger,' he says, 'is that corn shucked?'

FROM THE BACKWOODS, USA

Vance Randolph tells how one time there was a fellow name of Tolliver, and he married the widow Jenkins. Him and her got along pretty good, only she was always a-talking about what a fine man her first husband was. Everything she said was God's truth, too. But that didn't keep Tolliver from getting mighty tired of hearing about it, morning, noon and night.

Tolliver was a fellow that never talked much, but when he did say something everybody paid attention. One Sunday there was a crowd of people come over for dinner, and most of them was his wife's kinfolks. After they had eaten, the folks just set around on the porch, a-belching and picking their teeth. They was all talking, of course, and pretty soon Tolliver's wife begun to brag on her first husband. The other folks chimed right in, and everything she said they would answer 'That's right,' just like a bunch of deacons hollering 'Amen' at a revival.

Tolliver didn't say a word all this time, but finally he cleared his throat, and everybody stopped talking to look at him. 'Yes, Mister Jenkins was a fine man,' says he. 'I reckon we're all sorry Mister Jenkins went and died.'

Abroad – Past and Present

Zee French And Others

LUCKY PIERRE

Pierre is a famous gigolo who has made love to women from all over the world. One has just travelled to France expressly for this purpose.

'And now, Madame,' said Pierre, 'I am going to kiss you on ze breasts.'

She giggles as Pierre does so.

'Now, Madame, I am going to kiss you where you never 'ave been kissed before.'

'Where's that?' she asks.

'On ze navel,' Pierre answers.

'Oh,' says she, dismissing the thought, 'That's not new. I've been kissed on the navel before . . .'

'From ze inside?'

LUCKY PIERRE AGAIN

Once a woman came all the way from the States just to get some special loving, you know, from lucky Pierre, in his own way, you understand.

He kissed her on the forehead and she moaned and groaned, and then he kissed her on the lips and she made more and more noise, and then on the navel, and just then Pierre heard another noise, a little noise she made, from below.

Pierre smiled and said, 'Quiet, jealous one, you are next!'

IN OLD TIME FRANCE

In old time France, the children's tutor in a rich family laid everyone in the house – the mistress, the nurse, the maid, and then the two boys who were his pupils.

When the father heard of this, he summoned the tutor. 'Since you have horizontalized everyone in my house – and may it do you a lot of good! – there will be no exceptions. You're going to have to take me too!'

METTERNICH ON TALLEYRAND

When told that Talleyrand had died, he remarked, 'I wonder why he did that.'

LATE DATE IN PARIS

Keeping a girl up until the *oui* hours of the morning.

IN NAPOLEON'S TIME

When a French officer captured a Russian one, the Russian sneered haughtily at him.

'We Russians fight for our honour, but you French fight only for money!'

'Why not?' returned the Frenchman. 'After all, each of us fights for what he needs most.'

ESTABLISHING PRECEDENCE

The family of the Duc de Levis-Mirepoix hold one of the oldest and most important French titles. It dates back to the ninth century.

The family claim to descend from the sister of the Virgin Mary, and when the members of the Levis-Mirepoix family pray, they are said to say, 'Ave Maria, ma Cousine.'

IN OLD SPAIN

A man buys four handsome donkeys at a fair. He mounts one of them and returns to his house.

On the way he counts his donkeys: one, two, and three. He forgets to count the one he is riding.

He arrives at his house and tells his wife, 'I have just bought four beautiful donkeys in the market place this morning, and now I discover only three!'

His wife stares at him in amazement, and replies, 'How strange! You see only three while I see five.'

In The Beginning

THE WORLD'S FIRST JOKE?

A cave-woman came running to her husband.

'Og!' she called out to him. 'Something terrible has just happened! A sabre-toothed tiger has gone into my mother's cave and she's in there. Do something! Do something!'

Og looked up from the mastodon drumstick he was gnawing and said, 'Why should I do something? What the devil do I care what happens to a sabre-toothed tiger?'

FIRST FABLE?

A lion, a donkey and a fox had been out hunting, and the kill had been very good. So when the sun began to set, the three of them paused to rest.

The lion said, 'Friend donkey, divide the kill into three parts, one for each of us.'

The donkey did so, producing three piles of almost miraculously equal size.

The lion promptly leapt on the donkey and killed him. Throwing his body on the rest of the kill, he said, 'Friend fox, divide the kill into two parts, one for each of us.'

The fox promptly shoved all the bodies together except for the corpse of one crow, which he put to one side. He said, 'Friend lion, have this heap for your half, and the dead crow will be my half.'

The lion smiled broadly and said, 'Well done, friend fox, but who taught you to divide so cleverly into equal halves?'

'The dead donkey,' said the fox.

THE BOSS

When God made man, there was only one, and the various parts of the body argued about who should be the boss.

The hands said they should because they did the work for man.

The feet thought they should because they took the man to where he could do the work and get food.

The heart thought it should because it pumped the blood that allowed the food to be digested by the stomach and reach the body.

The brain said, 'No. I have to send all the signals to get each of you to do your jobs; therefore, I am the boss.'

The ass-hole said, 'I'll show you all who is the boss,' and clogged up the works.

After a few days the stomach ached . . .

The feet could not carry the body . . .

The hands were practically helpless . . .

The heart was about ready to stop pumping the blood . . .

The brain's signals were being ignored . . .

And even today, this teaches a MORAL:

You don't have to be a brain to be a boss . . . just an ASS-HOLE.

From Ancient Greece

SPARTA

For centuries, the Spartans of ancient pagan Greece told the story of a heroic boy who had been on a military mission. While scouting in the forest for the enemy, he was attacked by a fox. Lest the enemy be alerted, the boy made no sound.

The fox had bitten through his side, when, still silent, the boy at last reached his own camp. He stumbled to his commander, saluted him, and died.

So we see the stupidity of following the rules too closely, of doing what one is taught and sacrificing one's self.

Because this story shows us that there are indeed fox-holes in atheists.

SPARTA AGAIN

A stranger in Sparta asked about their customs. 'Why do your women walk about in the streets unveiled before marriage, but veiled after marriage?'

The Spartan answered, 'Before marriage they have to catch a husband; afterwards their husbands have to keep them.'

IN ATHENS

In the fifth century BC a talkative barber asked, 'How do you like your hair cut, sir?'

'In silence.'

And when a master said to his slave, 'Damn you, boy,' the slave replied, 'After you, sir.'

Ancient Rome

IMPERIOUS JULIA

Julia, the daughter of Augustus, was asked why she did not model her conduct after the example of her father's frugality.

She answered, 'He forgets that he is Emperor; I remember that I am an Emperor's daughter.'

JULIA AGAIN

The same Julia was the centre of a discussion with her friends who knew how wantonly she behaved. The friends marvelled that all her sons looked like her husband, Agrippa.

She said, 'I take no passengers aboard unless the hold is full.'

From Olde England

THE LANDLORD OR THE SIGN?

A lady and her two daughters took lodgings at an inn in Piccadilly, at the sign of 'The Cock and Leather Breeches'. But the lady was always embarrassed when she had to direct anybody to her lodgings, because the sign was such an odd one.

The lady, being a very good sort of woman, sent for the landlord who was a jolly young fellow. She told him she liked him and his lodgings very well, but she would be obliged to quit them because of his sign. She was ashamed to tell anyone what it was.

'Oh, dear madam,' said the young fellow, 'I would do anything rather than lose such good lodgers. I can easily alter the sign.'

'So I think,' answered the lady, 'and I'll tell you how you may satisfy both me and my daughters. Only take down your Breeches and let your Cock stand.'

SCORING

A gentleman about town followed a woman because she had a gorgeous figure. But when he caught up with her, he saw her face, and found it was not up to his expectations.

He stopped and bowed. 'Lady, if I had liked you as well before as behind, I would have kissed you.'

'Kiss where you like, sir!' she said.

TWO CAN PLAY

An old woman gossip, self-elected supervisor of village morals, accused a workman of reverting to drink because she had seen his wheelbarrow outside the public house.

The workman made no defence, but that evening placed his wheelbarrow outside her door and left it there all night.

DR JOHNSON

One of Dr Johnson's landladies once asked him what he thought of the soup he was sipping.

'Good enough for hogs,' he replied.

'Shall I help you to a little more of it?' she retorted.

OLD TIME LONDON

Two friends, out for a walk, were discussing whether coition or defecation afforded the greater pleasure.

They saw a woman who had never been known to refuse a man. 'Let's ask her,' said one. 'She's an expert in both matters.'

'She's the last one who should adjudicate!' exclaimed his friend. 'She's made love far more often than she has done the other!'

A COURTIER AND A SCHOLAR MEET

A Courtier proud walking along the street
Happened by chance a scholar for to meet.
The courtier, who minded nothing more than place,
Said to the scholar, meeting face to face,
'To take the wall — base men I'll not permit!'
The scholar said, 'I will,' and gave him it.

TAKING THE WATERS

Two ladies just returned from Bath were telling a gentle-man how they liked the place and how it agreed with them. The first had been ill and found great benefit from the waters.

'But, pray, what did you go for?' said he to the second.

'Wantonness,' replied she.

'And pray, madam,' said he, 'did it cure you?'

FROM THE FIFTEENTH-CENTURY

A Master of Arts is not worth a Fart
  Except to be in schools.
A Bachelor of Law is not worth a straw
  Except he be among fools.

ON A MAID'S LEG

Fair Beatrice tucked her coats up somewhat high,
Her pretty leg and foot that men might spy.
Quoth one: You have a handsome leg, sweet duck,
Yes, two (said she) or else I have ill luck.
They're two indeed, I think they're twins (quoth he).
They are, and yet they are not, sir (quoth she)
Their birth was both at once, that I'll be sworn,
And yet betwixt them both a man was borne.

WHAT IS A MAID?

The Duke of Queensbury, a notable gambler and wencher, agreed to the terms he had to pay a procurer to have consigned to him a young, inexperienced girl fresh from the country, a paragon of innocence.

But when she was brought in, to his inexpressible surprise he recognised an old acquaintance.

'By Gad!' he said. 'Why, I ruined you three months ago!'

'No, Your Grace,' she replied, 'you did not. I takes more ruining than you think!'

From Zee Old-Time East

IN THE HAREM

The Sultan sits in the midst of his wives. He looks thoughtful; the wives look worried.

The chief wife is complaining. 'You've been very cold to us lately. Are there others?'

ANOTHER HAREM

A doctor has been called for the Sultan who seems rather glum.

'Nothing to worry about, Your Highness,' the doctor says. 'I'll have you back in bed in no time.'

THE HODJA, WISE MAN OF TURKEY

The Hodja's wife was weeping at the bedside of the Hodja, her seventh husband.

'Who will take care of me when you die?'

The Hodja replied, 'Your eighth husband.'

THE DOCTOR PAYS THE FEES

It was the custom in China for the doctor to be held responsible for the health of his patients. One doctor had the misfortune to treat a young boy who died. The parents threatened to sue, and the doctor had to agree to hand over his own son.

Later on, the doctor lost another patient – the servant of a client. To compensate, he gave in exchange his own only servant.

One night, a neighbour knocked on the doctor's door, crying out, 'Oh, doctor, my wife is having a baby. Please come and attend to her at once!'

By now the doctor was wary. 'Ah, the blackguard!' he exclaimed to his wife. 'I know what this one wants – he wants you!'

A FOOLISH BIRD

A guest at dinner sat tight and showed no sign of leaving. At length the host called his visitor's attention to a bird sitting on a nearby tree, and said, 'Our last course has been served, but if you wait until I cut down that tree, I will catch the bird, have it cooked, and tell the butler to bring up some wine. What do you say to that?'

'Well,' replied the guest, 'I expect that by the time the tree is down, the bird will have flown.'

'No, no,' said the host, 'that is a foolish bird, and doesn't know when to go.'

FOUR GENERATIONS

When his son obtained a princedom, a Chinese duke was overjoyed. The son, who had expected his father to be offended that he now outranked him, was astonished at his father's reaction, and asked him to explain.

'Well, you see,' replied the father, 'your father has now gone one better than my father.'

And From Zee New-Time East . . .

The Pearly Gates, etc.

RARE PRIZE?

At the Pearly Gates the Archbishop of Canterbury and the leading Bible Belt evangelist are at the head of the queue.

The Duty Archangel is checking their credentials, when suddenly an attractive blonde, smiling and confident, marches past them and greets St Peter. He beams at her. He leaves the others waiting while he sees that she is comfortably settled in.

Watching this, the two clergymen are a bit amazed. Why should she get the red-carpet treatment, in view of the services rendered by themselves?

St Peter explains. 'Down on earth she drove a fast sports car, cut in and out of traffic and went through red lights. Gentlemen, she scared the devil out of more people than the two of you put together!'

CONFESSION

An Irish cricketer died and went to Heaven. At the Gate the white-robed saint asked if there was anything he wished to mention.

'Well, to tell the truth, there's one thing that has bothered me for years.'

'And what is that, my son?'

'Some years ago when Ireland played the MCC at Lord's, I opened the innings for Ireland. I survived an appeal for call at first slip, though I knew I had touched the ball. I stayed on and scored 295.'

'Did Ireland win?' asked the saint.

'Yes. By an innings and 27 runs.'

'Think nothing of it, my son. All is forgiven. Enter the Gates!'

The cricketer was delighted. 'Oh, thank you, St Peter!'

'By the way, I'm not St Peter. I'm St Patrick,' smiled the saint.

THE BIG NEWS

An angel breaks a wing and flitters, flitters, flitters down and lands on Earth right in front of a bar. All the fellows drinking there come out and start talking to him.

'Are you really an angel? Are you real?'

'Yes, I'm real, really. But I broke a wing and I happened to fall here.'

'Are you really from Heaven?'

'Yes, I am. All angels are from Heaven.'

'Tell us about it! Uh, have you seen – God?'

'Oh yes.'

'Tell us about God!'

'Well, for one thing, She's Black.'

Pope John XXIII, a farmer's son, said there were three ways by which a man is destroyed. 'They are, by drink, by women, and by farming,' he said. 'And my father chose the least exciting of the three.'

GAMES IN HEAVEN

Two baseball fans who were real old-timers used to talk to each other every day about the games and teams of the past. They were sure their heroes were in Heaven, and as they grew very old they made a pact to find out if this was true.

They agreed that the first of them to die and go to Heaven would get word to the other.

Soon after that, one of them died.

Shortly afterwards, the other somehow received a message from him. 'It's just as we thought! All the great batsmen are here!'

'Tell me more!' begged his friend.

'Oh, I will, I will. Which would you like first, the good news or the bad news?'

'The good news!'

'Well, they're all up here, Babe Ruth, Lou Gehrig, all the champs. And they choose a team and play a Heaven championship game every weekend!'

'Wonderful!'

'Now for the bad news. You ready?'

'Yes.'

'You sure?'

'Yes.'

'You're scheduled to pitch next Saturday.'

In the beginning God created the heaven and the earth.

2 And the earth was without form, and void; and darkness was upon the face of the deep. And the spirit of God moved upon the face of the waters.

3 And God said:

$$\oint \vec{H} \cdot \vec{d\ell} = I + \frac{\partial \phi_D}{\partial t}$$

$$\oint \vec{E} \cdot \vec{d\ell} = -\frac{\partial \phi_B}{\partial t}$$

$$\oint \vec{D} \cdot \vec{dS} = Q$$

$$\oint \vec{B} \cdot \vec{dS} = 0$$

and there was light.

MORE GAMES

God, the Angel Gabriel and Jesus go out for a game of golf. The Angel Gabriel tees off at the first hole – and gets a hole in one. Jesus is next to play; to takes a mighty swipe at the ball and sends it twice around the course before it finally comes to rest in the hole.

God then plays. The ball rolls 4 feet from his club and stops. It is then picked up by a rabbit, which bolts 100 yards down the fairway before being caught up in the talons of a golden eagle, which carries it 300 feet in the air before dropping it, ball and all, into the hole.

God looks modestly at his fingernails.

Staring up at him in dismay, Jesus says, 'Bloody hell, Dad! It's only a game!'

MORE GOLF

At one time, the golf course at a famous club was haunted by the ghost of a member who had died some years before.

One day this ghost appeared before a player and said, 'Would you like to win your championship match today?'

'Certainly,' said the player. 'If I win this match I'll be one of the tops.'

'Well, I can help you,' said the ghost, 'on one condition. You must promise never to marry, or even to have a girlfriend, for the rest of your life.'

'Done!' said the player.

And thanks to the help of his supernatural friend, he won easily and from then on broke all the club records.

As he was happily walking towards the clubhouse at the end of the games, the ghost appeared to him again. 'Just for the records at the Pearly Gates,' said the ghost, 'could I have your name?'

'Of course,' replied the player. 'It's Father O'Flanagan.'

HEAVENLY QUIZ

Why do Baptists object to premarital sex?
Because it can lead to dancing.

Who was Joan of Arc?
Noah's wife.

BEFORE DIVORCES

A wedded man came to the Pearly Gates and claimed the heritage he deserved as wedded. St Peter opened the gates, bade him come in, and said he was worthy to have his heritage because he had had much trouble, worthy to have a crown of glory.

A second man came and claimed heaven. He told St Peter he'd had two wives.

St Peter said, 'Come in, come in, for thou art worthy to have a double crown of glory, for thou hast had double trouble.'

Soon there came a third. He told St Peter he had had three wives and wished to come in.

'What!' cried St Peter. 'You've been delivered twice of your trouble, and entered it willingly a third time! Go thy way to Hell, thou shalt never come to Heaven.'

HEAVEN

The Earth has just blown up in nuclear warfare. Only half the sphere is left, and over the jagged remnant is a huge mushroom cloud.

Above the ruins hovers the robed and bearded figure of God.

He speaks.

What does he say?

'Well, there's six days' work shot!'

HELL

An inveterate gambler died, and although he was admitted into Heaven, he soon found himself bored.

Eventually he asked St Peter if he could take a look 'at the other place'.

'I'm afraid it's impossible,' said St Peter. 'If you go down there you won't be allowed back.'

'But I only want to have a look around.'

So St Peter agreed to issue him with a special pass which would let him stay for just twenty-four hours.

Off went the gambler to have a look around Hell, and the first thing he saw was a group of old acquaintances playing poker. However, they refused to admit him to the game because he had no money.

'I'll soon fix that,' he said, and off he went down one of the corridors. Ten minutes later he was back, flourishing a big roll of £10 notes.

'Where did you get all that money?' asked one of the others.

'I sold my pass,' replied the gambler.

MORE HELL

Three sinners met in one of the circles of Hell on their way to the lower levels. They got to talking and asked each other what misdemeanours had brought them there.

One said, 'I was a Jew while I was on Earth, but alas, I had a weakness. For ham sandwiches. So you see what happened to me.'

'I was a Catholic,' said the second, 'and we could eat all the ham sandwiches we wanted. But I was too inclined towards the ladies, alas! Adultery was my chief sin, and that's why I am here.'

The third remained silent. The other two turned to him. 'What about you,' they asked. 'Why are you in the hot place?'

The third said firmly, 'I am an Atheist; this place is not hot; and I am not here.'

MOST HELL

In Hell, two old men recognized each other. 'What are you doing here?' asked one. 'You were so good on Earth! Why? Why in Hell? I don't understand. You gave good charity. You gave good will – everything. What are you doing here in Hell?'

'Well,' said the other, 'I only died last night. The portals of Heaven were wide open for me. I walked in. They gave me a lyre and I started to play the lyre on a cloud. It was like a lovely summer evening.

'All of a sudden, what do I see? A beautiful chariot all gold and emeralds and on top of it a muscular man. His blonde long hair reached to his wings. He had a shining pink toga and a shining blue toga. And beautiful blue eyes.

'I couldn't resist saying it. I called him "Queer!".

'But he was the Holy Ghost!'

FRIENDS, "How do you stand with the Lord?"
"What do you mean, 'Which One?'?!"

For those of you who are unsure about your current faith or belief
system, we offer a viable alternative. We would like to introduce
the newest breakthrough in contemporary religion:

YES, FRIENDS, GODS LIKE THESE CAN BE YOURS

when you join: # the God of the Month Club

INCLUDED IN THIS FANTASTIC OFFER: Each month you will receive
                                    complete rituals of the
current God &/or Goddess of the month, including what (or whom)
to sacrifice. (All monetary sacrifices should be sent to our
Board of Directors.)

As an introductory sample GOD OF THE MONTH, we are offering your
choice from the list below. Simply send your choice with a mere
$2 to our Board of Directors. If you are satisfied with our Club,
simply send us $10 for each additional God you choose. If not,
you can cancel at any time. (However, if you wish to cancel, do
so promptly. We are not responsible for the actions of wrathful
Gods; some get <u>very</u> annoyed if They arrive at your doorstep and
find They are unwanted.)

A complete book of available Gods &/or Goddesses will be sent
to you with your introductory sample package. This is virtually
an encyclopaedia of religions, and by itself more than worth the
price of the introductory offer.

********************* -GODS OF THE MONTH- ********************

```
(    _Allah_ - Instructions on taking hostages included         )
*                                                               *
(    _Amon-Re_ - For that Old Time Religion                      )
*                                                               *
(    _Kali_ - Practice Thuggee!  Be the first on your block to be )
*            the last on your block!                            *
(                                                               )
*    _Herbie_ - Including a gross of lollipops--with the rare    *
(             cinnamon included!                                )
*                                                               *
(    _Solipsi_ - For those who believe you are God yourself!     )
*                                                               *
(    _Sum Dum Goy_ - Our resident guru, for those who prefer gurus )
*                                                               *
(    _Mammon_ - A.K.A. "The Golden Calf"--the All-American Religion*
*                                                               )
(    _Aphrodite_ - Goddess of Love--No explanation needed        )
*                                                               *
(    _Asmodeus Mogart_ - Equal time for demons                   )
*                                                               *
(    ...And many more available after trial offer.              )
```

****

Please note: It is suggested that care be exercised in choosing the
              order in which you select your gods, as some require
              virginity. Also, no fair picking virgin sacrifices
              under the age of consent. (As in Victorian England
              the age of consent may be considered to be twelve
              years of age.)
Also--check local state laws, or for a small additional fee our
legal department will assist you.

Yes--we are looking for people who like to prey. Read on →

Jehovah...Venus of Willendorf...Lord of the Flies...Hairy Krishna...Mithras...Tiamat...Tammuz...Satan...Red-Letter...Manitou...

Arære...Zeedru...Cvanda...Nland/Artemis...Eris/Discordia...Moon Old Sun...Odin...Yog-Sothoth...Daingod...Aldones...

...Isis...Lugh...El-Ron Hu-Bard...Lazarus Short...Foster...Hecate...
John Dillinger...Triton...Gwalchmai...Nhuni-i...Poseidon...Isis...
Sehmet...

HEAVEN AGAIN

St Peter was dividing the crop of newly-arrived souls for easier processing.

'All right, you men, come up here. Just the men, please. We'll take care of the women later.'

The men being at hand, he said, 'How many of you are married men here with your wives? Good. All those of you who are the boss in your family, line up over here. The hen-pecked ones in that other line, there.'

The line of the hen-pecked formed immediately and grew bigger. The other line was non-existent until one lone man appeared, a little fellow with a weak chin and a frightened look on his face.

St Peter paused to look at him. 'Are you aware that this is the line for those men who are boss in their family?'

'Yes, sir.'

'Are you sure you belong here?'

'I have to be,' he said. 'My wife insists.'

AT THE PEARLY GATES

A certain Pope died. To his chagrin he found himself at the rear of an interminable line at the Gates.

'What's all this?' he asked St Peter who came by on one of his periodic inspections. 'I was Pope, you know. Do I really have to wait with all these common people?'

'I'm afraid so,' said St Peter. 'You have to be processed strictly in order of earthly demise. And what with earthquakes and wars and epidemics, I'm sorry to say you couldn't have come at a worse time.'

So struggling with impatience, the late Pontiff stood in line with thieves and vagabonds and rogues and Labour and Tories. Slowly, very slowly, the line shuffled forward, but it was a good three years by earthly time before His Holiness finally reached the check-in desk.

The recording angel had his pen poised to take down the career details from the Patriarch of the West, Vicar of Christ, Servant of the Servants of God, Bishop of Rome, etc. etc., when a shabby old man clutching a battered leather bag shuffled straight past and in through the Gates.

'Who was that?' demanded the deceased Pope. 'For three years I, the Pope of Rome, have waited to get this far, and yet you let that scruffy-looking individual go in without let or hindrance!'

'But that's God Himself!' explained the recording angel. 'He likes to go down to Earth once in a while to play doctor.'

ALL IS VANITY

Sam was the ugliest man in the world. Because of this, God and his angels decided to give him one wish, to make things up a bit.

Sam thought for a minute and decided that since the handsome fellows all got rich and had all the women, his one wish was that he would become the most handsome man in the world.

Boom! It happened!

Sam was so overjoyed he immediately ran out into the street where, very unfortunately, he was hit by a big lorry.

As he lay in the street on the verge of death, he screamed out, 'Why, Lord? Why? After you've gone through the trouble of making me handsome, I don't even live an hour to enjoy it!'

All of a sudden a voice from the sky rang down. 'Well, hell, Sam, I didn't recognize you!'

PROTESTANT WORK ETHIC

Lonely, I stood at the Pearly Gates
My face so scarred and grey.
I stood before the Man of Fate
For admission to the 'fray'.

'What have you done?' St Peter said
'To gain admission here.'
'Worked for Volvo, Sir,' I said
'For many and many a year.'

The Pearly Gates swung open wide,
As Peter touched the Bell.
'Inside,' He said, 'and choose your Harp
You've had your share of Hell.'

SHEATH-BURSTING ROMANCE!!!

MALCOLM BENNETT & AIDAN HUGHES

BRUTE!
Colossal, work-hardened men! Wild untameable women!
Savage, unbridled passion! Raw and erotic tales of
gut-wrenching drama and suspense!!

BRUTE!
Romance, cruelty and religion! Sport, crime and agriculture!
Horror, western and football!!

BRUTE!
The cult comic of the 80s now unleashed in paperback!

'**Unmatched in contemporary British comic art**'
CITY LIMITS

'**Tough and dirty**' **THE FACE**

'**Graphic, gruesome and hilarious**' **BLITZ**

'**In future all novels will be written like this**' **TIME OUT**

0 7221 1565 2   CULT/GENERAL FICTION   £1.95

RICHARD TURNER & WILLIAM OSBORNE

The sensational, futuristic super-shocker based on the hilarious radio series

Edward Wilson was a low-profile wimp until he suddenly found himself on prime time TV lolling open mouthed in the arms of the pneumatically buxom page-three star Tabafa Minx. Eyes agog, his girlfriend was furious. She'd *kill* to be a famous media mega-star like her Ed . . .

But then so would everyone else in 1998. For the British economy is irrevocably ravaged and instant stardom is the only means to instant cash. And when lucky Edward ends up trapped in the bombed-out wreckage of a baby Berger bar with a comatose nubile at his feet, filofax-toting PR man Gordon Blank knows he'll fit the jackpot. But he needs a death to up the pathos quotient. So he calls in the bulldozers. And Edward realises that, literally this time, he's going to be splashed all over the nation's front pages . . .

Combining the outrageous inventiveness of Robert Sheckley with the hilarity of Douglas Adams, *1998* is a riotous rip-cord of savage social comment!

0 7221 6581 1   SCIENCE FICTION   £2.99

Deadly gamesmanship in the ruthless world of
championship golf . . .

BULLET HOLE

Keith Miles

For Alan Saxon, the British Open Championship is a cruc
tournament. He's on top form and being tipped as a winn
But his game is rudely interrupted by the appearance of a
young, pretty golf groupie who ends up naked and dead o
his bed. And she's not the only problem. Someone wants
Saxon out of the Open. But who? Which of his competito
is so desperate to win that he'll stop at nothing? Not eve
murder . . .

'A golfing Dick Francis'
GOLF WORLD
'A compelling story . . . as thrilling as holing a
25 yard putt'
DAILY MAIL
'A racy novel . . . good fun'
GOLF WORLD

0 7221 6039 9   CRIME   £2.95

A THOROUGHLY LEWD COLLECTION
OF EXCEEDINGLY RUDE RHYMES!!

Ribald, ingenious, hilariously blue – this
side-splitting selection of bawdy limericks will
have you reeling with riotous laughter and
mirth-filled merriment. There's Adam
complacently stroking his madam . . . Irene
who made an offering quite obscene . . . Hyde
who fell down a privy and died . . . the young
fellow of Kent who had a peculiar bent . . . the
brainy professor named Zed who dreamed of a
buxom co-ed . . . and many, many more!

0 7221 1297 1   HUMOUR £1.95

A selection of bestsellers from Sphere

FICTION

REDCOAT	Bernard Cornwell	£3.50 ☐
WHEN DREAMS COME TRUE	Emma Blair	£3.50 ☐
THE LEGACY OF HEOROT	Niven/Pournelle/Barnes	£3.50 ☐
THE PHYSICIAN	Noah Gordon	£3.99 ☐
INFIDELITIES	Freda Bright	£3.99 ☐

FILM AND TV TIE-IN

RUN FOR YOUR LIFE	Stuart Collins	£2.99 ☐
BLACK FOREST CLINIC	Peter Heim	£2.99 ☐
INTIMATE CONTACT	Jacqueline Osborne	£2.50 ☐
BEST OF BRITISH	Maurice Sellar	£8.95 ☐
SEX WITH PAULA YATES	Paula Yates	£2.95 ☐

NON-FICTION

THE COCHIN CONNECTION	Alison and Brian Milgate	£3.50 ☐
HOWARD & MASCHLER ON FOOD	Elizabeth Jane Howard & Fay Maschler	£3.99 ☐
FISH	Robyn Wilson	£2.50 ☐
THE SACRED VIRGIN AND THE HOLY WHORE	Anthony Harris	£3.50 ☐
THE DARKNESS IS LIGHT ENOUGH	Chris Ferris	£4.50 ☐

All Sphere books are available at your local bookshop or newsagent, or can be ordered direct from the publisher. Just tick the titles you want and fill in the form below.

Name _____

Address _____

_____

Write to Sphere Books, Cash Sales Department, P.O. Box 11, Falmouth Cornwall TR10 9EN

Please enclose a cheque or postal order to the value of the cover price plus:

UK: 60p for the first book, 25p for the second book and 15p for each additional book ordered to a maximum charge of £1.90.

OVERSEAS & EIRE: £1.25 for the first book, 75p for the second book and 28p for each subsequent title ordered.

BFPO: 60p for the first book, 25p for the second book plus 15p per copy for the next 7 books, thereafter 9p per book.

Sphere Books reserve the right to show new retail prices on covers which may differ from those previously advertised in the text elsewhere, and to increase postal rates in accordance with the P.O.